LEADERSHIP AS A CALL TO SERVICE
The Life and Works of Hildegard of Bingen

Leadership as a Call to Service

The Life and Works of Hildegard of Bingen

Christine Cameron

Connor Court Publishing

Connor Court Publishing Pty Ltd

Copyright © Christine Cameron 2015

ALL RIGHTS RESERVED. This book contains material protected under International and Federal Copyright Laws and Treaties. Any unauthorised reprint or use of this material is prohibited. No part of this book may be reproduced or transmitted in any form or by any means, electronic or mechanical, including photocopying, recording, or by any information storage and retrieval system without express written permission from the publisher.

PO Box 224W
Ballarat VIC 3350
sales@connorcourt.com
www.connorcourt.com

ISBN: 9781925138870 (pbk.)

Cover design by Ian James

Printed in Australia

Contents

Acknowledgements vii

Foreword by international Mezzo Soprano
Linn Maxwell Keller ix

PART ONE: Setting the Context

1. Introduction 3
   Hildegard as Servant Leader 4
   Servant Leadership 6
   Service and Leadership 8
2. Profile of St Hildegard of Bingen 12
   Early Life 12
   Benedictine Nuns 14
3. Origin of the Title – Doctor of the Universal Church 19
4. Honoured by the Church 29
   Criterion – Eminent Doctrine 30
   Criterion – Sanctity of Life 34
   Criterion – Approval by the Pope
   and/or his General Council 36
5. The Ten Core Characteristics of Servant Leadership 38

PART TWO: The Ten Core Characteristics of Servant Leadership applied to the Life and Works of Hildegard of Bingen

6. Listening 55
7. Empathy 64

8. Healing 75

9. Awareness 87

10. Persuasion 98

11. Conceptualisation 110

12. Foresight 123

13. Stewardship 133

14. Commitment to the Growth of People 144

15. Building Community 156

PART THREE: A Snapshot Comparison of four women & Conclusion

16. A Snapshot Comparison of Four Women 171

    St Hildegard of Bingen

    St Catherine of Siena

    St Teresa of Ávila

    St Thérèse of Lisieux

17. Conclusion 197

    Glossary (Doctors of the Universal Church) 202

    References 204

Acknowledgements

Acknowledgement is made of the incredible support and outstanding contribution of Dr Dan Riley my former doctoral thesis supervisor who has spent many hours and months assisting me with the research and editing of this book. Dan has been involved in every aspect of the book's creation and I owe him a debt of gratitude for his ongoing commitment to the life and works of St Hildegard of Bingen.

Special acknowledgement and appreciation go to the international Mezzo Soprano Linn Maxwell Keller who so kindly agreed to write the Foreword to this book and whose outstanding portrayal of Hildegard in a performance in Sydney, Australia, in May 2015 to celebrate the 25th Anniversary of the Australian Catholic University was a delight to all in attendance for Linn's acting, music and singing are superb.

I acknowledge all past and present members of the Benedictine Order throughout the world for it is through their dedication and patient perseverance over centuries that one of their own, Hildegard of Bingen, has been included in the catalogue of saints with her 'equivalent canonisation' in 2012 and later that same year being honoured with the title of *Doctor of the Universal Church*.

My deepest appreciation goes to my husband John Cameron for his continued love and support over many months of wondering if my 'project' on Hildegard was ever going to be completed and his kind reminders in recent months when other commitments became pressing to find the time to complete my work on Hildegard so that my research could be shared with others. I also acknowledge my mother Maureen Mary Daly, a woman of tremendous strength and compassion who taught me to value people and to love learning.

As with my first book, "I acknowledge the work of Robert Greenleaf (1970), whose seminal work on servant leadership has inspired all who undertake the role of leadership in a spirit of service to others and I acknowledge the work of [all servant leaders including] Larry Spears (1998) with his identification of the ten core characteristics of servant leadership which provided the framework and inspiration for this book" (Cameron, 2012).

I owe a debt of gratitude to the authors referenced in this book; in particular, Pope Emeritus Benedict XVI, Barbara Newman, Sabina Flanagan, Carmen Butcher, Teri Degler and a special acknowledgement to Anna Silvas who so kindly shared her notes with me and to Joseph Baird whose book, *The Personal Correspondence of Hildegard of Bingen* (2006), was invaluable and used extensively during the investigation into the life and works of this great saint. I encourage all readers to access the works of these scholars whose research is second to none and whose efforts reflect their genuine love and affection for this extraordinary saint of 12th century Germany – Hildegard of Bingen.

Finally I thank Hildegard for her amazing contributions to the Church and to humanity. Her teaching, medicine and music are all just as relevant today as they were over 800 years ago. She is indeed a 'Light' and inspiration for our times.

Foreword

The book you are about to read provides a new paradigm for understanding the ministry of a twelfth-century cloistered Benedictine nun, St Hildegard of Bingen, the fourth woman doctor of the Church in light of twenty-first century servant leadership. Christine Cameron reveals to us the role of the servant leader as defined by Larry C. Spears (1998). She demonstrates how St Hildegard embodies each of the ten characteristics presented by Spears: listening, empathy, healing, awareness, persuasion, conceptualisation, foresight, stewardship, commitment to the growth of people, and building community. By examining the saint's life and writings, Cameron places Hildegard in the company of twenty-first century religious, educational and corporate leaders who shape and guide our own journeys. She then compares St Hildegard's servant leadership to that of the other three women doctors of the Church: St Teresa of Ávila, St Catherine of Siena and St Thérèse of Lisieux, whose theological teachings were deemed to have lasting value for all time, not just for the times in which they lived. Cameron's first book, *Leadership as a Call to Service* (2012) explores the then three female doctor saints using the grid Spears provides, and this second book seamlessly weaves the golden thread of servant leadership through the life and works of St Hildegard, now a member of this exalted company of saints.

Dr Cameron reminds us that St Hildegard was above all a product of her own society and culture in the twelfth-century German Rhineland. In order to fairly examine her servant-leadership characteristics we must first and foremost view her through her own lens, that is by examining what we know of the daily milieu in which she lived and served – her cloistered monastic life at Disibodenberg and later at her convents at Mount St Rupert and its daughter house in Eibingen where the modern Hildegard Abbey stands today. The Benedictine Rule served as the daily guide for worship and work. In these foundations Hildegard served as *magistra* (teacher), and considered her role as the leader and spiritual mother of her nuns to be her highest responsibility and her moral duty. In *Voice of the Living Light: Hildegard of Bingen and Her World*, John Van Engen writes, "Hildegard understood caregiving as leadership in a struggle for souls and bodies, and she herself experienced losses. Hers was no finishing school but a battleground", (cited in Newman, 1998:45). Her role of *magistra* thoroughly prepared her for leadership in the other arenas where she would publicly acclaim her theological and prophetic message.

St Hildegard's voice as servant leader permeates her own voluminous correspondence. In the nearly 400 extant letters and replies, we meet time and again with a woman who was sought out by popes, cardinals, heads of state, frustrated abbots and abbesses, as well as anonymous monks and lay people. Hildegard consistently urged her correspondents to stay the course, to seek God's will and to do the *right thing*. She treated each person with equal respect and dignity, and when necessary, called someone to account for inappropriate or unwarranted actions.

Since 2009 I have toured with my play, "Hildegard of Bingen and the Living Light," and I have met audience members all over the English-speaking world who long to know this saint more deeply. My play touches on a few of the many aspects of her amazing and multifaceted life: her initial papal confirmation as a reliable and orthodox visionary of the Church, her music, healing, conflicts with Church hierarchy and her prophecies. Yet there is so much more to St Hildegard's message and ministry! By meeting Hildegard as a servant leader through Christine Cameron's insightful work, we may enrich our relationship to her and to each other. This book will be our guide.

Linn Maxwell Keller

PART ONE

SETTING THE CONTEXT

1

INTRODUCTION

During his long pontificate (1978-2005) St John Paul II canonised hundreds of saints but proclaimed just one *Doctor of the Universal Church* – St Thérèse of Lisieux on 19 October 1997, the year that marked the anniversary of the centenary of her death. This proclamation brought to thirty-three the total number of candidates conferred with the doctoral title by the Catholic Church during the course of its extensive history. And it was not until 2012 that this honour was again bestowed on a saint of the Church with significant changes occurring within the global community during the intervening years including the dawning of the third millennium, the emergence of the twenty-first century and the election of a new Pope – Benedict XVI, following the death of St John Paul II in 2005.

On 27 May 2012, Pentecost Sunday Pope Benedict XVI announced to a crowd of pilgrims gathered in St Peter's Square his intention to confer the title of *Doctor of the Universal Church* upon Saint Hildegard of Bingen and Saint John of Ávila. The Proclamations for the two candidates occurred on 7 October 2012 with both saints being raised to the doctoral ranks (Benedict, 2012a:6). This was an unprecedented move by the Pope and heralded a departure from the norm. For not since the proclamations of St Teresa of Ávila in September 1970 and St Catherine of Siena in October 1970 had two doctors been declared within the same year.

Nevertheless the candidates, St John of Ávila and St Hildegard of Bingen, fulfilled the three essential criteria of eminent doctrine, sanctity of life and acceptance and approval by the Pope and/or his General Council. Then in February 2015, Pope Francis, who had been elected Pope in March 2013 following the *unexpected* resignation of Pope Benedict XVI that same year, proclaimed his first Doctor – the Armenian tenth century 'mystic and poet', St. Gregory of Narek (*Apostolic Letter*, 12 April 2015) thus bringing to thirty-six the total number of *Doctors of the Universal Church*.

The purpose of this book is to focus on the second of the three most recent doctors – St Hildegard of Bingen. The process will involve applying the ten core characteristics of servant leadership as identified by Larry Spears (1998:4-6) – listening, empathy, healing, awareness, persuasion, conceptualisation, foresight, stewardship, commitment to the growth of people and building community – to the life and works of this fourth woman doctor of the Catholic Church. The following chapters will reveal that the servant leadership approach is most effective in that its focus on the leader as servant fulfils the mandate of Christ (Matthew, 20:26-28): "whoever wishes to be first among you must be your slave; just as the Son of Man came not to be served but to serve, and to give his life a ransom for many."

Hildegard as Servant Leader

Hildegard was born at the end of the first century in the second millennium AD and when writing from the perspective of the second decade of the third millennium caution is warranted. Christopher O'Donnell (1997:28) recommends that for contemporary readers to do justice when approaching classical texts the use of hermeneutics should be employed to better understand the meaning of the texts (Cameron, 2012:128). Hermeneutics is an approach which Michael Patton (2002:114) maintains informs qualitative inquiry, "It reminds us that what something means depends on the cultural context in which it was originally created as well as the cultural context with which it is subsequently interpreted."

Richard Marius and Melvin Page (2007:35; cited in Cameron, 2012) caution those engaged in historical research to be "on guard against reading today's definition into yesterday's words." They further add: "We must rely on evidence from the past such as memories of those who were there and objects from that time to guide us as we tell the story. But all these are mere records, subject to many interpretations and subject also to the tricks memory plays even on eyewitnesses. We can never relive the event exactly as it happened. The evidence for past events is therefore always incomplete and fragmentary" (p. 4).

Sabina Flanagan (1995:11) endorses these comments by stressing the importance of examining Hildegard's work:

> [within] its historical context. Failure to do so has contributed to misreadings of Hildegard as an exponent of Creation Spirituality, environmentalism, or feminism. Hildegard's views are best understood in the context of her own times and of her entire oeuvre [work], rather than being selectively quarried to support currently popular positions. Such treatment ultimately diminishes, rather than enhances, her reputation. She is remarkable enough in her own right.

Consequently in order to investigate the ways in which the ten core characteristics of servant leadership are reflected in Hildegard's life and works it is important to adopt a hermeneutic approach – this enables the texts to be studied with respect to the time, circumstances and culture of the era in which the texts are written. Richard Palmer (1969, cited in Patton, 2002:114) maintains that "To make sense of and interpret a text is important to know what the author wanted to communicate, to understand intended meanings, and to place documents in a historical and cultural context."

St Hildegard of Bingen was a product of her society, culture and time. And while acknowledging and respecting the historical and cultural context of twelfth century Germany it is emphasised that a cautious hermeneutical approach is adopted in this book – an approach that is also open-ended regarding the author's interpretation of the data that have survived through the centuries and which comprise Hildegard's legacy to the contemporary Church. It is important to remember that "Candidates [for the doctoral title] are meant to be 'doctors of the Church' not merely for their own times, but for all time" (Umberto Betti, 1988:282, cited in Steven Payne, 2002:27).

Servant Leadership

This book investigates Hildegard's role as a servant Leader. Robert Greenleaf first proposed the paradigm of servant leadership in 1970. Greenleaf had been interested in this concept of leadership after reading *The Journey to the East* by Hermann Hesse (1956). "Hesse writes of travellers on a journey, a mystical journey and describes their experiences and relationships with each other" (cited in Christine Cameron, 2012:14). The travellers become dependent on the servant Leo who provided invaluable service to the group: "Leo was one of our servants … He helped carry the luggage and was often assigned to the personal service" of the leader (Hesse, 1956:77).

During the course of the journey Leo appears to be the cohesive element of the group maintaining unity, balance, peace and serenity and when Leo disappears the group becomes fragmented and disjointed and there is infighting and rebellion. The group eventually disintegrates and the journey is discontinued. "One particular member of the group wanders aimlessly for years searching for peace and for Leo. The climax of the tale is when Leo is found and is discovered not to be a servant but the leader of the group, the President" (Hesse, cited in Cameron, 2012).

The origins of servant leadership can be traced back to antiquity and eastern origins (Cameron, 2012). While in the west it can be traced to biblical times and in particular to the person of Jesus Christ, whom Bennett Sims (1997:16) refers to as "the prototype of the servant leader." And as Hildegard's life and works are investigated in this book it becomes apparent that servant leadership is perhaps just one of many approaches to leadership that could be attributed to her leadership practices. For example two such approaches that come immediately to mind are spiritual leadership and transformational leadership. Greenleaf (cited in Anne Fraker and Larry Spears, 1996:125), asks us to "recognise spirit as an essential ingredient of leadership" and Michael Hackman and Craig Johnson (2009:103) describe transformational leadership as being "empowering and inspirational; it elevates leaders and followers to higher levels of motivation and morality."

In fact a more contemporary approach to leadership where leaders are encouraged to have a global perspective is, in our post modern society, being referred to as the ecology of leadership (Julie Boyd, 2012). In other words a leadership paradigm where leaders reflect on the realities of the twenty-first century, taking into account "the challenges that transcend the complex systems within the natural environment" (ibid.), and develop an "awareness of the interconnectedness of all realities – spiritual, cosmic and existential" (Fritjof Capra, cited in Spears, 1998:119; cited in Cameron, 2012). And while it is tempting to apply this twenty-first century concept of leadership to Hildegard whose many titles include that of a 'naturalist' (Flanagan, 1998), caution is again warranted regarding the drawing of conclusions from works "which are not apposite for our time" (O'Donnell, 1997). Flanagan (1995) stresses this with her emphasis that environmentalism as such would not have been a consideration in Hildegard's era.

Nevertheless Hildegard did respect creation and the environment. For example in Book One of Hildegard's *Physica*, which is described by Priscilla Throop as a 'Medical work', Hildegard states "with earth was the human being created. All the elements served mankind and, sensing that man was alive, they busied themselves in aiding his life in every way" (1998:9). There are additional references to ecology in Chapter 13 when the core characteristic of *Stewardship* is applied to Hildegard's life and works.

In sum, to attempt to investigate an almost infinite number of leadership paradigms is beyond the scope of this book whereas the servant leadership approach with its emphasis on service appears best suited to the leadership practices of a Benedictine nun who lived in twelfth century Germany and who is depicted through the following chapters as having lived a life of dedicated service to the Church.

Service and Leadership

The Second Vatican Council (1962-1965) promoted the Gospel's message of service. Service is a word "that occurs (in its Latin form, *servitium*) eighty times in the body of the text of Vatican II, 'especially in the constitutions on the Church and on the Church in the modern world'" (Notes cited in Joseph Komonchak, 2006:583; Cameron, 2012). According to Greenleaf (cited in Fraker and Spears, 1996:201), "The idea of servant is deep in our Judeo-Christian heritage. Servant (along with serve and service) appears in the Bible more than thirteen hundred times ... beginning with the book of Genesis." Interestingly one of the many titles of the Holy Father is that of *Servant of the Servants of God* (Cameron, 2014).

The concept of leadership is a phenomenon that has been studied extensively. Some questions regarding Hildegard's approach to leadership could include – what qualities are important for leadership and how did Hildegard possess those qualities that resulted in her acceptance of the mantle of leadership? To answer such questions perhaps it is important initially to respond to the basic question – What is Leadership?

Joseph Rost (1993:37-38) in his critique on leadership includes statements by Ralph Stogdill (1974) and Bernard Bass (1981) which attempt to define the origins of the terms *leadership* and *leader*. According to Rost, the research of Stogdill and Bass revealed: "the appearance of the word 'leader' in the English language as early as the year 1300." However, Bass (1981:7, cited in Rost, 1993:37-38) maintains that the word 'leadership' did not appear until the first half of the nineteenth century in writings about political influence and control of the British Parliament (cited in Cameron, 2009).

Rost (1993:39-44) is critical of the lack of a suitable definition for leadership by scholars and practitioners of leadership. John Antonakis et al. (2004:4) maintain: "100 years of leadership research has led to several paradigm shifts and a voluminous body of knowledge ... As stated more than four decades ago by [Warren] Bennis (1959:259-301), [but] 'probably more has been written and less is known about leadership than about any other topic in the behavioral sciences.'" Stogdill (1974:7, cited in Bass, 1981:11) states that "There are almost as many definitions of leadership as there are persons who have attempted to define the concept" and Ian O'Harae (2007:7) emphasises Gary Yukl's (2002) assumption that leadership has "defied the odds and remained an elusive, somewhat enigmatic notion" (cited in Cameron, 2009).

Rost (1993) believed that many scholars and practitioners did not define leadership because they thought that everyone knew intuitively what it meant or more precisely "they do not know how to define it." However, early in the twenty-first century Rost (2005:1) stated in an interview with Russ Volckmann (Publisher and Editor of the *Integral Leadership Review* Journal): "They [scholars and practitioners] didn't want to define it [leadership] because they wanted to have the freedom of writing about leadership any way they wanted" (cited in Cameron, 2012). Volckmann (2012) adds:

> It is well known in leadership studies that several hundreds of definitions have been offered for the term *leadership* and

that none has been selected as a basis for building a field of study ... This certainly calls for an approach that can create some order out of the chaos while enhancing our ability to appreciate leadership occurrences in varying contexts and the qualities and relevance of diversity and differences.

Volckmann emphasises the importance of the contextual nature of leadership: "[Rost] understood the importance of context for any attempt at definition. Here I take this a step further and suggest that *every definition of leadership is by its nature contextual and is true, but partial.* Each has something of value to offer in the practice, development and study of leadership" (2012). Volckmann proposes rather than providing a definition for Leadership per se it might be best to focus on the concept from a different perspective. He refers to the work of Donna Ladkin (2010:1) who suggests that: "we need to change the questions we ask from 'What is leadership?' to 'How do we understand the phenomena of leadership?'"

According to Volckmann "This is very much a step in the right direction. Leadership, however we construe the term, is going to appear and be different in a tribal setting, a kingdom, a church, a business or a community. Even within such broad categories, there will be differences in the expectations and practices of individuals in those human systems" (2012). Thus a leader may find that there are "similarities and differences in all theories and models of leadership however much depends on the context and the attitudes, values and behaviour of the leader in ensuring effective leadership practices, regardless of which leadership theory is espoused" (cited in Cameron, 2012).

In the context of this book the initial cultural setting for leadership is a faith-based environment within a monastery at Disibodenberg in the twelfth century and the wearer of the mantle of leadership is Hildegard, a member of a religious order. Hildegard succeeded the anchoress Jutta of Disibodenberg as *magistra* (prioress) within the community of nuns upon the death of Jutta in 1136. Hildegard, was selected with "the unanimous consent of the sisters … though she resisted it with all her strength; she was constrained to assume the office of prioress by the command of the Abbot and the insistence of her sisters" (Anna Silvas, 1998:111-112). And according to Silvas (1998:113) "She was raised, despite her reluctance, to the service of holy leadership."

In this book then the ten core characteristics of servant leadership, as identified by Spears (1998): listening, empathy, healing, awareness, persuasion, conceptualisation, foresight, stewardship, commitment to the growth of people and building community are applied to the life and works of St Hildegard but firstly it is important to share some of the saint's background with the reader. Hence the following chapter profiles the life story of this *remarkable* saint of Bingen.

2

PROFILE OF ST HILDEGARD OF BINGEN

Early Life

Few details are available but it is believed that Hildegard was born at Bermersheim in Germany around 1098 close to the dawn of the 12th century. The family name is unknown and indeed there is very little information recorded on Hildegard's family except that her parents were of noble lineage and were quite wealthy and owned property. Hildegard was the tenth and youngest child of Hildebert and Mechtild and as such when she was born her parents offered her as a 'tithe' to God (Silvas quoting Guibert a monk and priest known to Hildegard, 2012:7) so that she would live her life in dedicated service to him. Pope Benedict in his Apostolic Letter proclaiming Hildegard a *Doctor of the Universal Church* (2012a:1) states that "at the age of eight she [Hildegard] was received as an oblate at the Benedictine Abbey of Disibodenberg, where in 1115 she made her religious profession."

Scholars differ on details regarding the age of Hildegard when she was admitted to the monastery, her experiences prior to the entry and whether she was admitted as an oblate or enclosed within the monastery. According to Emily Sutherland (2010:1) "Hildegard of Bingen's age, when she was enclosed in a small stone edifice attached to the Abbey of Disibodenberg sealed from the world with its snares and temptations, has still to be satisfactorily resolved." Sutherland defines 'oblation and enclosure' which she maintains are 'separate entities':

> The conditions under which a child oblate was received into

a Benedictine monastery in the twelfth century is stipulated in the rule of St Benedict, Chapter 59. Having been offered to God by his or her parents the child would live within the monastery with the monks or nuns, and would be expected to participate as fully as possible in the monastic life. Enclosure would mean living in isolation, sealed within an enclosed cell attached to a church or monastery, leading an ascetic life of intense prayer, with minimal contact with the outside world or the monastic community (ibid.).

Flanagan (1998:65) maintains that Hildegard objected "to the indiscriminate oblation of children … children, she says, are not to be constrained to enter religion against their will but should be asked, on reaching the age of understanding, whether they wish to follow this course." James Hamilton (2006:1) posits that the loss of a parent can have a traumatic effect upon a child. And in fact Hildegard lost both her parents upon her entry to the monastery. Though Hildegard gained a substitute mother in Jutta Von Sponheim her experiences growing from childhood to adulthood within the walls of a monastery could well have contributed to the enigmatic personality that was to become the adult woman and future saint and doctor of the Catholic Church!

Hildegard was a sickly child and though she lived until her eighth decade her health was always fragile. She is said to have had visionary experiences and at a very young age was placed in the care of a "consecrated widow Uda of Gölklheim" (Pope Benedict XVI, 2010a:1) who was also the teacher of Jutta von Sponheim, who was the "daughter of the widowed Countess Sophia and the sister of Meinhard, Count of Sponheim" (Silvas, 2012:7). Hildegard's father Hildebert is said to have been "closely connected with the Counts of Sponheim" (Silvas, 1998:2) who were Jutta's family. In articles and books on her life Jutta is sometimes referred to as *Blessed* however according to personal communication received from Rome (19 March

2015) via the Benedictine sisters in Germany, "Jutta is called 'beata' [Blessed] like hundreds of other holy people before and after her time, but was never officially beatified."

Flanagan notes that Hildegard's parents placed her in the care and under the guidance of Jutta who was six years her senior "The life they chose for her was that of a companion to Jutta, daughter of Count Stephan of Sponheim, who lived in a cell near the church of the Benedictine monks at Disibodenberg" (1995:1) Jutta taught Hildegard the rudiments of reading and some writing though Flanagan, a scholar of Hildegard's works maintains that Hildegard "was always quick to point out how limited her formal education had been, emphasizing that she had been taught by an ... [unlearned woman] and, consequently, that any insight she gained into theological or secular matters was divinely inspired" (Flanagan, 1995:2).

According to Silvas (1998:44) it was in 1112 when Hildegard was in her fifteenth year and Jutta was twenty that they were received with another companion (also referred to as Jutta) at the Benedictine monastery at Disibodenberg where Jutta had been previously persuaded to undertake the life of a consecrated anchoress (a holy woman) living in confined quarters – a small room (cell) called an anchorage that "was often attached to the wall of a church" (Middle Ages Website, 2015). It was in such a setting that Hildegard, Jutta and their companion were 'solemnly enclosed' in a section of the monastery at Disibodenberg with the ceremony being performed by Bishop Otto of Bamberg (Silvas, 1998).

Benedictine Nuns

During those early years of Hildegard's 'confinement' Jutta was the *Magistra* (Prioress) in the monastic monastery at Disibodenberg. The nuns followed the rule of St Benedict and the community flourished under Jutta's leadership. According to Silvas (1998:44), "The holy

Jutta, daughter of Count Stephan, was also the *Magistra* in Christ of the virgins at Disibodenberg ... and under her, their numbers greatly increased. Many nobles of the regions offered their daughters for the service of our Lord Jesus Christ under her guidance." Silvas refers to the increasingly cramped conditions of the confined quarters of the growing band of women – for they were "enclosed separately in a strict and well-walled custody. No men had access to them except the Abbot" (1998:44).

In 1136, after some twenty-four years of service to the Church and to the community, Jutta died and Hildegard (though initially reluctant to assume the mantle of leadership) was "constituted *Magistra*" under the Abbot Cuno (Silvas, 1998:45) also written 'Kuno' (Flanagan, 1998:226). Inspired by Hildegard's leadership the numbers of eager young women wanting to join the community grew and it wasn't long before the increasingly confined conditions become intolerable for the growing band of keen, spirited young women. Hildegard realised that she needed to seek more suitable accommodation to settle her growing community and as time passed extenuating circumstances soon forced the issue. For example Benedict (2010a:1) cites the influence of the "increasing number of young women ... [and] the dominating male monastery of Disibodenberg" as reasons for the nuns' decision to leave. Another more important explanation was that Hildegard believed that she had received a 'divine command' to relocate her nuns elsewhere (Barbara Newman, 1990:13).

Silvas (2012:9) tells us that initially Hildegard resisted the summons from the Lord "undergoing much psychosomatic illness in the process" for since the death of Jutta she continued to experience the visions that had assailed her in girlhood and that now 'afflicted' her in womanhood. And apparently during those early years Jutta and the monk Volmar (who was later to become Hildegard's secretary, staunch friend and confidant) were the only two who were privy to Hildegard's visions. However in 1141, some five years after the death of Jutta, Hildegard received a vision unlike any others she had received – a form of spiritual awakening which is further explored in Chapter 9 when the core characteristic of *Awareness* is applied to Hildegard's life and works.

According to Teri Degler (2007:4-5) the vision had a tremendous impact and changed Hildegard's life forever:

> When the Abbess Jutta died in 1136 Hildegard's life seems to have unfolded uneventfully enough for about five more years until she had a direct experience of the 'living light' itself which was quite different from the 'reflection of the living light' that she had envisioned continually since childhood. This profound vision literally transformed her consciousness ... [T]he voice in the vision commanded her 'to say and write' what she 'saw and heard' in her visions ... At first Hildegard refused to do so. She had kept quiet about her mystical visions for years ... In the Preface to *Scivias* she explains that this reticence arose out of a combination of humility, self-doubt, and concern for 'evil opinions' ... She soon fell ill, she says "pressed down by a scourge of God" and remained so until she finally began to write down her visions and compile them into what would eventually become *Scivias*, a 600-page book that contained both detailed description of her visions and interpretations of what they meant for humankind.

The significance of the vision was that Hildegard "was instructed to leave St Disibod [the monastery at Disibodenberg] ... and found a new convent on the site of a ruined Carolingian Monastery near Bingen" (Newman, 1990:13). However this plan met with vehement objections from the Abbot Cuno, who according to Degler (2007:8) "flatly refused to give her [Hildegard] permission to leave. The monks, naturally, did not want to lose the prestige associated with Hildegard, the land and money the new postulants were bringing to the monastery, or the gifts from the faithful that Hildegard's fame as a visionary were attracting." And according to Silvas (2012:9), "It would be difficult to overstate the sheer difficulties involved in this break with the monks of Disibodenberg: the legal wrangles, the financial worries, the barrage of criticism and so forth. But Hildegard resolutely pushed it through." In addition opposition to the plan did not just come from the monks for many of the nuns "were [initially] loath to leave their comfortable surroundings for a desolate wilderness" (Newman, 1990:13). Flanagan elaborates:

> [T]o go from lush fields and vineyards and the comforts of home to a desert place devoid of amenities and "to move from a place where they wanted for nothing to such great poverty" ... these were not girls who'd come from poverty and want, they were nobly born and wealthy ladies who had never known any form of hardship. And to make their decision to follow Hildegard even more difficult, the monks refused to allow the nuns to take the dowries (the money and lands they had originally brought with them on their entry into the convent at Disibodenberg) with them to Rupertsberg (cited in Degler, 2007:8-9).

The pressure and stress of trying to please everybody resulted in Hildegard suffering a near death experience (a paralysing illness) and her health only improved when she decided to submit herself to the will of God and accept that God was calling her to relocate her community of nuns. Hence as a result of her visionary experiences Hildegard decided to leave the monastery at Disibodenberg. She used "her family connections to secure the land [where she was to settle her community] and ... [the fact of her] miraculous 'charismatic illness' to persuade the abbot that her departure was the will of God" (Newman, 1990:13). The Abbot relented and with his permission, albeit given reluctantly, Hildegard with a small band of her faithful followers (probably less than twenty nuns) moved to Bingen where "Making use of the alms of the faithful, she built a monastery for herself and her sisters there on the hill of the Confessor Rupert" where she spent the remainder of her days (Silvas, 1998:45).

After settling at Rupertsberg Hildegard was to found a second convent in 1165 which was established at Eibingen near Rüdesheim in Germany (just across the Rhine from Bingen). Hildegard spent her later years travelling around the countryside engaged in preaching and teaching the clergy and laity. On 17 September 1179 Hildegard of Bingen died in Rupertsberg at the age of eighty-one.

The next chapter discusses the origin of the doctoral title that has been conferred on the 36 candidates who have been proclaimed *Doctors of the Universal Church*.

3

ORIGIN OF THE TITLE –
DOCTOR OF THE UNIVERSAL CHURCH

The doctoral title has its origins in the history of the early Church. Authors who have attempted to define this ancient and 'enigmatic' title include Kenneth Woodward, John Fink, Bernard McGinn, and Lawrence Cunningham. Now, Woodward (1990:160) describes the title as being, "honorific ... bestowed by popes for saints of exceptional learning and/or knowledge of the spiritual life." Fink's (2000a:xi) definition is similar to that of Woodward; he refers to the doctors as Christian writers who, because of the sanctity of their lives and the legacy of their eminent doctrine, have been formally recognised by the Church (cited in Cameron, 2009).

McGinn (1999:4) describes the term "doctor" as coming from the Latin *doctrina* which he explains "signifies the act of teaching, instructing or training of any kind." McGinn recounts how the early pagan Romans used the term to depict highly skilled teachers, such as Plato. McGinn also acknowledges the influence of Tertullian, a North African and Christian theologian of the second century. Apparently Tertullian "used the term doctor both to refer to priests and also to indicate how all Christian teachers depend ultimately on the Holy Spirit" (ibid.). McGinn explains that Tertullian referred to the apostles of the New Testament as doctors who were teachers and that he (Tertullian) believed that their infused knowledge came from the gifts of the Holy Spirit, and that the apostles handed down this teaching legacy to future generations of Christian teachers (McGinn, 1999).

This handing on of the Gospel message by the Apostles is referred to as the *Apostolic Tradition* (Catholic Catechism, 2000:24; cited in Cameron, 2009).

Cunningham maintains that: "The concept of the title 'Doctor of the Church' has a long and somewhat complicated history. The early patristic writers often spoke of the 'fathers and doctors' of the church. The term 'doctor' (Latin: *docere*, to teach) was used to describe the eminent teachers of doctrine in antiquity" (2005:87; cited in Cameron, 2009). Christopher Rengers refers to the derivation of the title from the "Latin: *docere*, to teach" and states that the title of doctor "designated anyone whose knowledge qualified him [or her] to teach" (2000:xi).

Doctor and *teacher*, this concept of a Christian teacher is reinforced in sacred scripture. Payne (2002:5-7) explains: "Although the expression 'doctor of the church' is found nowhere in the bible, words related to teaching and learning occur often throughout its pages, as they do throughout the literature of the ancient world." Payne also states that the title of teacher was often given to Jesus in the scriptures because: "Catholic tradition acknowledges God as the ultimate teacher, the source of all knowledge and wisdom, and Jesus as the very incarnation of this supreme knowledge, and wisdom, both the teacher and the teaching itself" (2002:5-7; cited in Cameron, 2009).

Payne maintains that, "doctors are Christian teachers" who share in the teaching ministry of Jesus Christ (2002:26). McGinn also promotes the concept of Jesus as teacher by providing scripture references where Jesus is referred to as rabbi/teacher (1999:2). Payne refers to the fact that the term teaching is used "many times in the New Testament, most frequently in the Gospels, and is identified as one of the most characteristic features of the ministry of Jesus" (2002:6; cited in Cameron, 2009).

McGinn (1999:2) reinforces the role of the Holy Spirit as teacher,

"Jesus promises his followers [to send] another counsellor and protector to teach them after he departs: 'The Paraclete, the Holy Spirit, whom the Father will send in my name, will teach you everything and remind you of all that I have said (John, 14:26).'" McGinn and Payne both emphasise that the Holy Spirit is teacher and doctor who infuses Christian teachers with knowledge and who is Christ's legacy to those who share in his teaching ministry:

> If we take the message of John's gospel seriously, the doctor of the church is always the Spirit sent in Jesus' name to the community of love symbolized by those gathered in the upper room at the Last Supper: all subsequent teaching is rooted in the Holy Spirit as the living inner source of the instruction delivered to humanity through Jesus Christ, the Incarnate Word (McGinn, 1999:2).

Christian teachers and writers who lived in the first century of the Church include the Evangelists – Matthew, Mark, Luke and John, who wrote the Gospels; and Paul who wrote the Epistles (Fink, 2000a:xviii). During the fourth century, Christianity became more widespread after the conversion of the Roman Emperor Constantine. As the Church grew, so also did the number of bishops. McGinn (1999:2; cited in Cameron, 2009) writes of the growing importance of the teaching office of a bishop:

> The development of titles and terms expressing positions of leadership and teaching authority in the early Christian gatherings, or churches (Greek – Ekklesia), is complex and still only partly understood. Pre-eminence was given to the apostles, the twelve members of Christ's inner circle, but Paul boldly ascribed the same title to himself on the basis of the appearance of the Risen Jesus to him, commissioning his preaching to the gentiles … the term bishop (episkopos, literally 'overseer') appears in the New Testament, where it seems to be used interchangeabl[y] with 'priest'.

Struggles, debates and the threat of heresies were characteristic of the *climate* of the early Christian church, which emphasised, "the power of the bishops as the true expositors of the Christian faith and the leaders of the community" (McGinn, 1999:3). The bishops organised councils to discuss problems and to determine guidelines according to tradition and to orthodox Christianity. McGinn states that bishops still continue in this role in the contemporary Church, indeed: "ever since, at least in the older Christian denominations, [they] bishops have been seen as holding the most authoritative official teaching position in the Church" (ibid.). However in the early Christian Church, the role of teacher was not just the exclusive right of bishops:

> Bishops did not act alone in teaching and leading their communities. A variety of other officials, mostly male (priests, deacons, catechists, etc.) but sometimes females (e.g., deaconesses) worked with them in instructing and governing each ekklesia. This broad penumbra of office indicates that the role of teacher, even as an official title, cannot be restricted to bishops (McGinn, 1999:3; cited in Cameron, 2009).

Now during its first millennium the Church has, according to Fink:

> recognized three categories of outstanding Christian writers: the Apostolic Fathers; the Fathers of the Church; and the Doctors of the Church ... The Apostolic Fathers were Christian writers of the first and second centuries whose writings were derived from Christ's Apostles ... the fathers of the Church were theologians and writers of the first eight centuries who were known for their learning and holiness (2000a:xi - xii).

The Fathers of the Church are known as the patristic (from the Latin: *pater* – father) writers. These men were members of the Eastern and Western Churches. Eight of the fathers are recognised (by tradition) as doctors of the Church. These eight comprise the four Fathers from the west (in no particular order): Gregory the Great, Augustine of Hippo, Jerome, and Ambrose; and the four fathers from the east (in no particular order): Athanasius, John Chrysostom, Gregory of Nazianzen and Basil the Great (cited in Cameron, 2009). All with the exception of Jerome were Bishops, with Gregory the Great holding the position of Pope (cited in Jean-Yves Lacoste's *Encyclopedia of Christian Theology*, 2005a:446).

Following the recognition "by tradition" of the eight doctors of the eastern and western Churches, the first solemn proclamation of a doctor of the Church was that of St Thomas Aquinas, a Dominican priest, who lived in the thirteenth century, and who was proclaimed a *Doctor of the Church* by the Dominican Pope Pius V in 1567 (cited in Lacoste's *Encyclopedia of Christian Theology*, 2005c:446). The second doctor to be officially proclaimed was St Bonaventure (a Franciscan priest), who was proclaimed a Doctor of the Church in 1588 by a Franciscan Pope, Sextus V. It was during this year, that is in 1588, that a formal *proclamation* process for the doctoral title was established:

> In … 1588, the Congregation of Rites … articulated the criteria by which a person would qualify as a Doctor of the Church. In the eighteenth century, Prospero Lambertini (later Pope Benedict XIV) summarized those criteria in his now classic work on beatification and canonization … a potential doctor should be a person of conspicuous holiness, a teacher of eminent doctrine, and be so named either by papal decree or a recognized General Council of the Church (Cunningham, 2005:88; cited in Cameron, 2009).

There were thirty-three *Doctors of the Universal Church* at the beginning of the third millennium of the Catholic Church, seventeen of these doctors "lived in the first millennium" and the remaining sixteen doctors "lived in the second millennium" (Fink:2000a).

Prior to the relatively recent proclamations in 2012 and 2015, the last male doctor was St Lawrence of Brindisi, who was proclaimed a Doctor of the Church by Pope St John XXIII in 1959. Just over a decade later followed the proclamations of St Teresa of Ávila and St Catherine of Siena in 1970 and then in 1997, St Thérèse of Lisieux (cited in Cameron, 2009). On 7 October 2012 St John of Ávila and St Hildegard of Bingen were proclaimed doctors and in February 2015 Pope Francis proclaimed St Gregory of Narek a doctor bringing the total number of *Doctors of the Universal Church* to thirty-six (see Chapter 1).

In sum, doctors are those 'saints' who have been formally recognised and honoured by the church for their teaching as well as their spirituality. Doctors are ecclesiastical writers whose theology has influenced believers throughout the ages (cited in Cameron, 2012). McGinn (1999:20) states: "a doctor of the church is a person that the pope has officially recognised as possessing the sanctity of life and eminence of teaching that deserves public liturgical celebration."

The doctors, by virtue of their proclamation as doctors of the Church are 'public figures' and therefore subject to public scrutiny. Their theological contribution "must have some lasting or permanent value" and must be relevant for all time (Payne, 2002:27; cited in Cameron, 2009). A number of the doctors possessed excellent academic qualifications. For example, many had degrees and taught at universities. Other doctors were prolific writers and theologians who produced volumes of published works; and still others produced homilies, treatises, poems and songs. Such diversity in the *theological* contribution of the doctors reflects the changing needs of the Church. Payne (2002:30; cited in Cameron, 2009) maintains that:

> "[T]he church now has different intellectual and pastoral needs, and thus may require new kinds of doctors." The saints of modern times whose teachings ... have made the greatest

impact were rarely professional scholars. In particular, while the door is now open to women doctors of the universal church, given earlier academic restrictions placed upon them there will be few if any potential candidates from before the twentieth century that could be considered "systematic theologians" in the traditional sense, though they may offer a "teaching" which has proved enormously influential in the church's intellectual and pastoral life.

The theology of Teresa, Catherine and Thérèse (the three women doctors at the time Payne wrote his book) has been described as pastoral (Cameron, 2012). Now McBrien (1981:57) defines pastoral theology as one, "which seeks to understand the implications of faith for the actual situation of the Church, specifically for preaching, ministry of various kinds, counselling, and the like." Interestingly Pope St John XXIII directed that the Second Vatican Council which was held from 1962 to 1965 be pastoral in nature. Giuseppe Alberigo (cited in Komonchak, 2006:584) commented on the reaction of those who disagreed with the Pope's directive, "Clumsy attempts have proposed to interpret the pastorality of Vatican II as a sign of weakness in order to reduce the authority of its documents" and even when writing forty years after Vatican II, Alberigo (cited in Komonchak, 2006:584) recognises the relevance of pastoral theology for the contemporary Church: "the insight of John XXIII, which the great majority at the Council made their own and which was supported by Paul VI, is one of the most important contributions of Vatican II; it is a direction that deserves to be more deeply explored and is capable of fruitful development."

Whether the candidates for the doctoral title come under the category of systematic theologians or pastoral theologians or somewhere in-between if they fulfil the criteria they are eligible for consideration. For according to McGinn (1999:20; cited in Cameron, 2009), "All baptised Christians, under the inspiration of the Holy

Spirit are called to be doctors in so far as they believe and teach the faith by word and example to the best of their ability."

McGinn's comments imply that there is no gender bias when a decision is made to proclaim a doctor of the Church. However McGinn (1999:xi) quotes a British theologian (1967), who claimed that, "it would seem that no woman is likely to be named [doctor] because of the link between this title and the teaching office, which is limited to males." Ironically, it was just a few short years later in 1970 that Pope Paul VI made the unprecedented move of proclaiming St Teresa of Ávila, the first woman doctor of the Catholic Church and approximately a week later the Pope proclaimed St Catherine of Siena a doctor (cited in Cameron, 2009). There is very little recorded data listing reasons why Paul VI decided to declare Teresa and Catherine doctors, as McGinn (1999:18) queries:

> The most recent innovation in the history of the "doctores ecclesiae" has been the naming of three female doctors. Given how much has been written about the pontificate of Paul VI (1963-1968) it is odd that there has been little discussion of his initiative in elevating the first two women to the status of doctor, St Teresa of Avila and St Catherine of Siena.

Now as early as the second decade of the twentieth century, Pius XI studied and prayed over the documents presented by the Discalced Carmelites in their efforts to have their *mother* (St Teresa of Ávila) proclaimed a doctor. Though sympathetic to the request, Pius XI could not bring himself to change centuries of traditional practice. His response was to issue a statement of *obstat sexus*, meaning "her sex was an obstacle." While Pius XI was unwilling to prejudice the eventual outcome by his response, it did not deter him from deciding to leave prospective changes in traditional practices to his successors (*L'Osservatore Romano*, No. 40, 1970:12; cited in Cameron, 2012).

St Thomas Aquinas, a doctor of the Church (who was born in the first quarter of the thirteenth century) did not believe that women would ever be proclaimed doctors. St Thomas endorsed the precept of St Paul, which Payne (2002:16) recounts when he quotes from the homily of Pope Paul VI, given during the proclamation of St Teresa of Ávila as Doctor of the Church: "'Let women keep silence in the churches' [1 Cor 14:34]. This still signifies today that woman is not meant to have hierarchical functions of teaching and ministering in the Church." McGinn (1999:18; cited in Cameron, 2009) explains:

> Pope Paul VI did not believe that by proclaiming a woman as a doctor of the church that he was violating St Paul's precept … "Not at all," says the pope. "The title of doctor is not connected to the hierarchical function of the magisterium. Through baptism, women participate in the common priesthood of all the faithful. In such profession of faith," he continues, "many women have arrived at great heights, even to the point where their words and their writings have become lights and guides for their brethren."

Eminent doctrine (teaching) is a requirement for a candidate to be declared a Doctor of the Church, regardless of gender; so when women are proclaimed doctors they are fulfilling the criterion of eminence of teaching, but according to McGinn (1999:18) women are "not meant to have hierarchical functions of teaching and ministering in the church." Interestingly in his *Apostolic Letter* proclaiming St Hildegard of Bingen a *Doctor of the Universal Church* Pope Benedict XVI when listing how Hildegard fulfilled the criteria refers to Hildegard's "holiness and her eminent teaching" (2012a:para.7) and then when referring to her "equivalent canonisation" (see Chapter 4) the pope praises Hildegard as "a famous teacher of theology" (ibid.).

Hence by virtue of being raised to the doctoral ranks Hildegard of Bingen has fulfilled all three criteria. For example she has fulfilled the criterion of eminent doctrine, which is reflected in her eminent teaching. She has fulfilled the criterion of sanctity of life, which is endorsed by her "equivalent canonisation" and she has fulfilled the criterion of approval by the Pope and/or his General Council by the formal public ceremony of her Proclamation.

The Catholic Church has honoured Hildegard with doctoral status and in Chapter 4 the process that led to her proclamation is discussed and includes highlights of the extensive collection of works attributed to this extraordinary saint of Bingen.

4

Honoured by the Church

The proclamation of a *Doctor of the Universal Church* is the result of a process that involves the Magisterium or "teaching authority of the Church" (Richard McBrien, 1981:1249). The title is honorary and is awarded posthumously. As stated previously the Catholic Church defines doctors as those 'saints' who have been formally recognised and honoured by the Church. They are ecclesiastical writers whose theology has been influential throughout the ages and whose work, while remaining *orthodox* and *original* is relevant for the Church, not just during the lifetime of the doctor, but for all time (cited in Cameron, 2009).

Pope Benedict XVI proclaimed St Hildegard of Bingen a *Doctor of the Universal Church* on 7 October 2012. During his Homily on that special occasion the Pope reflected on the many gifts of this twelfth century German Benedictine nun:

> Saint Hildegard of Bingen, an important female figure of the twelfth century, offered her precious contribution to the growth of the Church of her time, employing the gifts received from God and showing herself to be a woman of brilliant intelligence, deep sensitivity and recognized spiritual authority. The Lord granted her a prophetic spirit and fervent capacity to discern the signs of the times. Hildegard nurtured an evident love of creation, and was learned in medicine, poetry and music. Above all, she maintained a great and faithful love for Christ and his Church (2012b:3).

The lengthy process to have Hildegard raised to doctoral status commenced in earnest on 6 March 1979. On that occasion Pope Benedict XVI, then Cardinal Archbishop of Munich and Freising, accompanied "Cardinal Joseph Höffner, Archbishop of Cologne and President of the German Bishops Conference … [and] the other Cardinals Archbishops and Bishops of the same Conference" as they submitted a request to Pope St John Paul II for Hildegard of Bingen to be declared a *Doctor of the Universal Church*. According to Benedict XVI, Hildegard of Bingen was a suitable candidate because "of her reputation for holiness and her eminent teaching." In the Apostolic Letter proclaiming Hildegard a Doctor of the Church Pope Benedict writes about the petition that was submitted by Cardinal Höffner, himself and the Archbishops and Bishops:

> In that petition, the Cardinal [Höffner] emphasised the soundness of Hildegard's doctrine, recognized in the twelfth century by Pope Eugene III, her holiness, widely known and celebrated by the people and the authority of her writings. As time passed other petitions were added to that of the German Bishops' Conference, first and foremost the petition from the nuns of Eibingen Monastery, which bears her name. Thus, to the common wish of the People of God that Hildegard be officially canonized, was added the request that she be declared a "Doctor of the Universal Church" (Apostolic Letter, 7 October, 2012a:6).

Remember for a candidate to be proclaimed a *Doctor* there needs to be evidence that the three essential criteria of eminent doctrine, sanctity of life and acceptance and approval by the Pope and/or his General Council have been fulfilled. By virtue of her elevation to the doctoral ranks Hildegard fulfilled the required criteria in the following ways.

Criterion – Eminent doctrine

This criterion is rather lengthy due to the many achievements and exceptional gifts of this extraordinary woman. In his Apostolic Letter

Proclaiming St Hildegard of Bingen, professed nun of the Order of Saint Benedict, a Doctor of the Universal Church Pope Benedict XVI (2012a:2) states:

> Her main writings are the *Scivias*, the *Liber Vitae Meritorum* and the *Liber Divinorum Operum*. They relate her visions and the task she received from the Lord to transcribe them. In the author's view her *Letters* were no less important; they bear witness to the attention Hildegard paid to the events of her time, which she interpreted in the light of the mystery of God. In addition there are 58 sermons, addressed directly to her sisters ... [and] a literary and moral commentary on Gospel passages related to the main celebrations of the liturgical year. Her artistic and scientific works focus mainly on music ... on medicine ... in the *Causae et Curae*, and on natural sciences in the *Physica*. Finally her linguistic writings are also noteworthy, such as the *Lingua Ignota* and the *Litterae Ignotae*, in which the words appear in an unknown language of her own invention...

Here Pope Benedict highlights Hildegard's impressive achievements which include her writings on theology and mysticism; her music; her extensive correspondence; her plays and poetry; her writings on medicine and science; and her creation of a 'new' form of Language. For the information of the reader these 'achievements' are now presented in greater detail.

Regarding Hildegard's Writings on Theology and Mysticism – her best known work – *Scivias* "short for *Scito vias Domini*, or *Know the Ways of the Lord*" (Newman, 1990:22) took Hildegard ten years to complete (1141-1151) and is the first work in what is often referred to as a trilogy of 'visionary writings' which record her mystical visions "which are first set down literally as she saw them, and are then explained exegetically [after analysis]" (Hart and Bishop, 1990). Together with the *Scivias* the other two works referred to by Benedict XVI (2012a) and that form the remainder of the trilogy are the "Book of Life's Merits" (*Liber vitae Meritorum*) written between 1158 and 1163 and the "Book of Divine Works" (*Liber Divinorum Operum*) written between 1163 and 1173.

Interestingly in addition to her writing Hildegard was a composer of Sacred Music. She composed songs, hymns and antiphons and a *Symphonia* – 'Symphony' which was composed around the year 1140. Historical data indicates:

> [Hildegard] wrote hymns and sequences in honor of saints, virgins and Mary. She wrote in the plainchant tradition of a single vocal melodic line, a tradition common in liturgical singing of her time. Her music is undergoing a revival and enjoying huge public success. One group, *Sequentia* [Ensemble for medieval music] ... [recorded] Hildegard's musical output in time for the 900th anniversary of her birth in 1998 (Fordham University Website).

And amazingly even now in the twenty-first century Hildegard's music is available for purchase through the relevant technology outlets and recordings of her music are available to download on computers and other digital software in a technological age that is far removed from the medieval times in which Hildegard lived and worked. For example in our contemporary era a CD recording of Hildegard's inspirational *Canticles of Ecstasy* described by some music lovers as a superb rendition of her work has been: "Performed to perfection by sequentia [Ensemble for medieval music] ... canticles of ecstasy transports the listener to an enchanted world of spiritual bliss" (Sequentia, BMG music, Inscription on back cover:1994).

Graham Abbott an Australian musician "who has conducted Australia's major orchestras, choirs and opera companies" explored the life and music of Hildegard of Bingen, in an Australian ABC FM broadcast on Sunday 28 September 2014. In his broadcast Abbott (ibid.) referred to Hildegard as a "remarkable woman ... [who] wrote music of luminous beauty." Nancy Fierro (1997:2) maintains that "Hildegard combined all her music into a cycle called The Symphony of the Harmony of the Heavenly Revelations ... [it is] In singing and playing music, we integrate mind, heart and body, heal discord between us, and celebrate heavenly harmony here on earth. According to Hildegard, this becomes our 'opus' – the epitome of good work in the service of God."

In regard to her *correspondence* – Hildegard was prolific with her letter writing. Carmel Posa (2012:1) maintains that Hildegard's "many letters indicate the range of her influence, from high to low estates. She wrote to kings, queens and popes, archbishops, abbesses and abbots, nuns and monks, laywomen and laymen seeking advice and giving it." Benedict (2012a:2) notes that "Her letters are ... numerous — about four hundred are extant [still in existence – though some historians record the number as around 300]; these [letters] were addressed to simple people, to religious communities, popes, bishops and the civil authorities of her time." Sr Philippa Rath OSB, in her article on "Hildegard of Bingen: Prophetess of her Time", states that "Hildegard gave a lasting expression to her prophetic ideas in her letters ... They are a testimony of fearless directness, radical truthfulness, admonishing concern, refreshing and humorous generosity, personal commitment for the poor and far-reaching political influence (concerning church-matters)."

Now Hildegard also wrote and produced plays and poetry including the "Play of Virtues" – *Ordo Virtutum* – a moral play (1150c). According to Throop (1998:3) the play "is written as a finale to *Scivias* ... The central character, the Soul, is torn between opposing arguments of the Devil and a choir of Virtues." In the film (biopic) on Hildegard (a video titled *Vision*, 2010) the play is performed in the convent with Hildegard's nuns acting the part of the virtues and the monk Volmar, Hildegard's secretary and close friend, performing the role of Satan. You may recall that Volmar accompanied the nuns when they relocated from Disibodenberg to Rupertsberg (Silvas, 1998:116).

Besides her "books on theology and mysticism ... [Hildegard] also authored works on medicine and natural sciences" (Benedict, 2012a:2). She wrote on medicine and nature in *Physica* and *Causae et Curae* which became her "Classic Works on Health and Healing" (Throop, 1998). Hildegard's trilogy of writings (referred to earlier in this chapter) are described as *visionary works* however not so her scientific works which apparently "don't contain any references to divine source or revelation." Newman (1990:17) explains: "Hildegard's prophetic self-awareness pervades all her writings except for her scientific works." Benedict (2012a:2) tells us that it was "Theological reflection [that] enabled Hildegard to organize and understand, at least in part, the content of her visions." Newman (1990:12) writes that "Hildegard's prophetic call came to her in 1141 in the form of a fiery light that permeated her whole heart and brain and gave her an infused knowledge of all the books of Scripture."

Hildegard's talents also included composing *Language* and *Letters* (1150) – she composed *Litterae ignota* [unknown Letters] and *Lingua ignota* [Unknown Language]. Flanagan (1995:4) writes that: "The latter is a glossary of some nine hundred invented words (mostly nouns), thematically arranged. They include the names of plants and herbs and so may have been related to Hildegard's scientific interests. Although the invented alphabet is used occasionally for titles in her correspondence." Degler (2006:5) refers to the *Language* and *Letters* as being incorporated into an "unfinished dictionary containing the definitions to some 900 words that appear to be from a completely unknown language." Indeed an impressive record of achievements!

Criterion – Sanctity of Life

This criterion was endorsed by Hildegard's canonisation though for Hildegard and her supporters this was not a straight forward process.

As early as 1227AD there were moves to have Hildegard canonised and over the centuries she was venerated as a saint but in reality the formal canonisation process was never completed until 10 May 2012 when she received what is referred to as "equivalent canonisation". Silvas (2012:1) quotes from the official report issued on 10 May 2012 stating that Pope Benedict XVI:

> [E]xtended to the universal church the liturgical cult in honour of Hildegard of Bingen, professed nun of the Order of St Benedict, born in Bermersheim, Germany in 1098 and died in Rupertsberg on 17 September 1179, enrolling her in the list of saints. This is a procedure which has been called "equivalent canonization", and it gives final recognition, on the pope's own motion and by his definitive judgment to the de facto veneration paid to Hildegard as a saint for many centuries, above all in her homeland, Catholic Germany, and in the Benedictine and Cistercian orders, and formally extends this veneration to the entire Church (L'Osservatore Romano Weekly Edition in English, no.20 [2246], Wednesday, 16 May 2012, p. 11).

In the Vatican newspaper *L'Osservatore Romano* (11 May 2012), Lucetta Scaraffia writes: "Hildegard of Bingen has finally been proclaimed a saint by the Church after centuries, even though she has been venerated as such since her death [Hildegard died in 1179], especially within the Benedictine Order to which she belonged." On 12 May 2012, *L'Osservatore* provided the following explanation for the term "equivalent canonisation":

> [W]hen the Pope enjoins the Church as a whole to observe the veneration of a Servant of God not yet canonized by the insertion of his [her] feast into the Liturgical calendar of the Universal Church, with Mass and the divine Office ... This judgement, however, is not expressed with the usual formula of canonization, but through a decree obliging the

entire church to venerate that Servant of God with the cultus reserved to canonized saints.

Pope Benedict XVI cites his reasons for granting Hildegard "equivalent canonisation":

> With my consent, therefore, the Congregation for the Causes of Saints diligently prepared ... [the necessary documentation] for the Mystic of Bingen. Since this concerned a famous teacher of theology who had been the subject of many authoritative studies, I granted the dispensation from the measures prescribed by article 73 of the Apostolic Constitution Pastor Bonus (Apostolic Letter, 2012a:6).

This section on the Criterion of Sanctity is quite brief as the mere fact that Hildegard has been added to the catalogue of saints fulfils the Criterion of Sanctity of Life.

Criterion – Approval by the Pope and/or his General Council

This final criterion was satisfied as a result of the formal and public proclamation/ceremony announcing Hildegard's doctoral status. In the Apostolic Letter proclaiming St Hildegard of Bingen a *Doctor of the Universal Church* Pope Benedict (2012a:6) concludes with the following declaration:

> In Saint Peter's Square, in the presence of many Cardinals and Prelates of the Roman Curia and of the Catholic Church, in confirming the acts of the process and willingly granting the desires of the petitioners, I spoke the following words in the course of the Eucharistic sacrifice: "Fulfilling the wishes of numerous brethren in the episcopate, and of many of the faithful throughout the world, after due consultation with the Congregation for the Causes of Saints, with certain knowledge and after mature deliberation, with the fullness

of my apostolic authority I declare Saint John of Avila, diocesan priest, and Saint Hildegard of Bingen, professed nun of the Order of Saint Benedict, to be Doctors of the Universal Church. In the name of the Father, and of the Son, and of the Holy Spirit."

Thus the Proclamations by Pope Benedict XVI of St Hildegard of Bingen and St John of Ávila in 2012 brought to thirty-five the total number of *Doctors of the Universal Church* and with the Proclamation of St Gregory of Narek in 2015 by Pope Francis the number has increased to thirty-six and includes thirty-two males and four females. The Glossary at the end of this book lists the names of all thirty-six *Doctors of the Universal Church*.

Hildegard of Bingen, though the most recent of the four women doctors to be proclaimed, was born close to the twelfth century and so precedes Catherine of Siena (fourteenth century), Teresa of Ávila (sixteenth century), and Thérèse of Lisieux (nineteenth century) in her life of service to the Church.

The following chapter includes a synopsis of the terms of reference for the ten core characteristics of servant leadership as identified by Larry Spears (1998:4-6) namely: listening, empathy, healing, awareness, persuasion, conceptualisation, foresight, stewardship, commitment to the growth of people and building community.

5

THE TEN CORE CHARACTERISTICS OF SERVANT LEADERSHIP

Servant leadership is an approach to leadership conceptualised by Robert Greenleaf in 1970 in an essay titled *The Servant as Leader*. This approach to leadership is based on Greenleaf's maxim that "the essence of leadership is service" (cited in Cameron, 2012). Hence the seminal work of Greenleaf (1970), on servant leadership and Spears (1998) with his identification of the ten core characteristics of servant leadership provided the framework for this study of the life and works of St Hildegard of Bingen in relation to the servant leadership paradigm. The following ten core characteristics are presented in the order in which they are identified by Spears (1998:4-5) and though each characteristic is listed separately all ten have similarities that often overlap (Cameron, 2012).

Listening

To listen is to engage in silence. Greenleaf (2002:31) tells us "One must not be afraid of a little silence. Some find silence awkward or oppressive, but a relaxed approach to dialogue will include the welcoming of some silence ... sometimes it is important to ask ... 'In saying what I have in mind will I really improve on the silence?'" According to Graham Bodie (2011) there are as many definitions of listening "as researchers studying the phenomenon." However if we look closely at the concept and how it is used listening would simply involve a connection with another person/s or with some form of technology; it could involve an emotional response (depending on the familiarity with the person/s engaged in the communication); and it would involve reflecting on what is being said or not said. Spears (1998) tells us that to listen effectively and to engage in active listening requires a balance of the body, mind, and spirit. He (1998:4) notes the importance of active listening which involves a person being attuned to what is said, how it is said, and being conscious of the needs and will of those engaged in the interaction (cited in Cameron, 2012:18).

Listening requires a profound knowledge and acceptance of self and strong interpersonal skills. This balance is found in reflective listening which occurs when listening to the "internal voice". Don DeGraaf et al. (2001) maintain that listening is "the foundation of servant-leadership … it is through listening that many of the other characteristics can be nurtured" for it is "When we listen, not just to what others are saying but also to our own internal voice, we create a mindset that fosters such characteristics as empathy, awareness, foresight, and commitment to others" (pp. 3-4; cited in Cameron, 2012).

Effective leaders listen and facilitate communication according to the needs of the group (David Rough, 2011). There is openness about the communication. Though Greenleaf (1977:17) advises: "Don't assume, because you are intelligent, able, and well-motivated, that you are open to communication that you know how to listen." Greenleaf (ibid.) reminds us of "that great line from the prayer of Saint Francis [of Assisi], 'Lord, grant that I may seek not so much to be understood as to understand.'"

Empathy

To have empathy is to have an acceptance of others. It is about giving and receiving trust. To be empathetic is to recognise and build on the strengths of others and accept their limitations, not reject them (Greenleaf, 2002:33-34). Having empathy for others draws an emotional response from a person that is based on feelings, experiences and being able to identify with the needs of the 'other' person. It is accepting others for the people they are with all their weaknesses and strengths. Roman Krznaric (2012) describes empathy simply as "the ability to step into the shoes of another person, aiming to understand their feelings and perspectives and to use that understanding to guide our actions."

Empathy encourages others to be the best they can be so that they in turn can lead (Greenleaf, 1977). Such a leader does not put self before others but shows understanding and compassion (James Hunter, 2004). However a servant leader is just one component of the whole – be it an organisation, a group or a team for it is the interconnectedness of all members working together that contributes to a successful working community (Spears, 1998).

Empathetic leaders listen empathetically and empathise with people known and unknown to them. They recognise the potential in others and empower and affirm them in their mission of service (Blanchard, 2007). Such leaders are compassionate and empathise with the needs of people and organisations and share vision and engage in mutual trust while listening empathetically to those in their care (Cameron, 2012). According to DeGraaf et al., such a leader is a servant leader, who is encouraged to develop the skill of empathetic listening for, "We need to go beyond simply listening: we need to be empathic with others. Empathy is the capacity for participation in another's feelings or ideas" (2001:5; cited in Cameron, 2012:20).

Healing

Greenleaf (2002) maintains that healing is developed through an awareness of the needs of the whole person, self and others – it is inclusive of the needs of all. Healing facilitates transformational change and wholeness (Blanchard and Hodges, 2003) and encourages a leader to take the time to withdraw to solitude for quiet prayer, reflection and self-healing (John Heider, 1985). Comparisons with 'the wounded healer' (Serge Daneault, 2008) are important. Daneault tells us that the term 'wounded healer' was used for the first time by Carl Jung in 1951, "Jung believed that disease of the soul could be the best possible form of training for a healer. In a book published days before his death, Jung wrote that only a wounded physician could heal effectively" (2008:1219). Contemporary definitions of the 'wounded healer' include those of:

> Religious writer Henri Nouwen [who] spoke of the wounded healer in terms of physical, spiritual and emotional well-being [and] Viktor Frankl, the famous physician, psychiatrist and survivor of the Nazi concentration camps, [who] wrote that to be ashamed of the experience of suffering is, essentially, to be ashamed of life itself; examining and owning the suffering in one's own life, he said, is the process by which we find meaning and hope (*University of Maryland Medical System*, 2013:2).

Daneault (2008:1219) adds "just like destiny or death, suffering is a fundamental human experience. For Frankl, if life has meaning, suffering must necessarily have meaning too. The way in which a person accepts his [or her] destiny and suffering provides his [or her] life with a profound sense of meaning."

Healing in our contemporary society involves a search for wholeness (Greenleaf, 2002:50) and as emphasised by Spears (1998) a servant leader needs to nurture and do what is required to restore the emotional, spiritual, intellectual, psychological and physical health of self and others (cited in Cameron, 2012:23).

Awareness

Awareness is cultivated through a leader being sensitive to the reality within and the reality without, and responding accordingly (Palmer, cited in Spears, 1998). It is an awakening to the spirit. Such a concept is explored in an article on Hildegard by Degler (2007:1) where the *awakening to the spirit* is described as reaching a "higher consciousness – an enlightened state attained only by the rarest of saints and mystics from spiritual traditions around the world." Degler (ibid.) cites the work of Gopi Krishna (a Kashmiri yogi and philosopher) stating that he believed that "the profound mystical experiences described by great saints and mystics – whether they called these experiences Samadhi, nirvana, enlightenment, or mystical union – were essentially the same."

> In yogic terms, such experiences are brought about by what is often called the awakening of kundalini. Although the word kundalini begs adequate translation, it is sometimes defined as an evolutionary energy/consciousness force … Gopi Krishna provided a list of the characteristics of kundalini awakening … Central to this awakening itself, he explained, is a profound mystical experience that includes an inexpressible sensation of divine love, bliss, or awe; an unfathomable vision of light, fire, or flames, and an overwhelming, all-encompassing awareness of the divine oneness of all things (Degler, 2007:1-2).

Such profound awareness is a gift given only to a few and according to Degler (2007:3) Hildegard of Bingen was one such visionary "not only because her degree of illumination was so great but also because she was both a true creative genius and a mystic blessed with divine revelation."

Awareness is being "in touch with the spiritual, existential and cosmic realities and sensing and responding to their interconnectedness" (Fritjof Capra, cited in Spears, 1998:119; cited in Cameron, 2012:24). Greenleaf (1977:254) wrote about spiritual awareness as a spiritual awakening, "[of] profound meaning for me, was the … belief that the highest level of religious experience is awareness of oneness with the mystery … the feeling of awe and wonder and amazement" (cited in Cameron, 2012:24). However Greenleaf (2002:41) does remind us that "Awareness is *not* a giver of solace – it is just the opposite. It is a disturber and an awakener. Able leaders are usually sharply awake and reasonably disturbed. They are not seekers after solace. They have their own inner serenity."

Awareness then for a leader is being able to anticipate and be conscious of what has to be done to maintain peace and harmony (Bennett Sims, 1997). It is about general awareness and awareness of self and others.

Persuasion

To persuade is to influence. According to Rough (2011) "Persuasion can take many forms but the result is still the same – a willing partnership designed to accomplish a shared vision of purpose." Persuasion involves a leader using the power of influence rather than the power of control or coercion (Greenleaf, 1977). Such a leader possesses an inner strength and charisma (Jay Conger et al., 2000) which are important attributes of the servant leader who needs to know when to assert himself/herself and when to be mentor, guiding, empowering and engaging others in shared and collective leadership practices (James Hunter, 2004).

Testimonials (Robert Hershey, 1993) and building consensus (Greenleaf, 1977) are considered persuasive tools. Hershey (1993:1) maintains that "if we are honest with ourselves … we cannot make people want to do … things but we might be able to persuade them to do so." Greenleaf (cited in Fraker and Spears, 1996:30) maintains that "Part of the success of consensus leadership is faith, confidence that the language exists that will provide the needed common ground if one will persevere and communicate this confidence to all involved." However leaders who are self-serving and who do not consider the needs of others will not usually engage in persuading others but will try to manipulate the situation/s to suit themselves.

Greenleaf (2002:116) quotes Lord Acton (former Professor of History at Cambridge University), "Power tends to corrupt and absolute power corrupts absolutely." DeGraaf et al. (2001:11) write of the "use and abuse of power." Leaders who abuse power abuse the followers they serve. Sims (1997:10) explains, "In the long run, no leader is privileged to 'Lord it over' anyone, in any system, because the universe itself is constructed to honor the freedom of the human spirit." Hence wisdom could be described as a persuasive tool for – "Wise power ... undergirds all that is, the velvet and steel in an enduring love: gentle enough to cradle the cosmos in patient care and strong enough to outlast and forgive all assaults on its compassion" (Sims, 1997:xi; cited in Cameron, 2012:27).

Pope Francis in his homily during his inauguration Mass in Rome in 2013 when celebrating the beginning of his papacy emphasised that "Leadership and power are really [all] about service." Christ's mandate is to serve:

> [W]hoever wishes to become great among you must be your servant, and whoever wishes to be first among you must be slave of all. For the Son of man came not to be served but to serve, and to give his life a ransom for many (Mk, 10:42-45).

In addition "The concept of dialogue is [also] an important component in the art of persuasion" (DeGraaf et al., 2001:12) and this would include the many letters written by Hildegard in the twelfth century of which over 400 are said to be still in existence now in the twenty-first century.

Conceptualisation

Conceptualisation is all about visualising the 'big picture' – having a vision for the future. It is developing critical skills when engaging in conceptual thinking (DeGraaf et al., 2001:14). Conceptualisation is about dreaming great dreams "looking at a problem ... from a conceptualizing perspective" and thinking "beyond day-to-day realities" (Spears, 1998:5). DeGraaf et al. (2001:13) cite Michele Hunt (1998) "who describes leaders who have these conceptualizing skills as *dream makers*. These people have the necessary insight and foresight to perceive the consequences of their actions." In 1993 Dr Martin Luther King Jr "outlined his vision in his 'I have a dream ...' by describing a world where his children 'will not be judged by the color of their skin but by the content of their character'" (Blanchard, 2007:33).

Conceptualisation involves planning and setting a purpose – the mission, for what needs to be done to achieve the end result – the vision. Greenleaf (1977:66) refers to a leader as having "conceptual talent" whereby s/he "sees the whole in the perspective of history – past and future – states and adjusts goals, analyses and evaluates operating performance, and foresees contingencies a long way ahead." Such a leader shares and serves the vision. Blanchard and Hodges (2003:68) state that these leaders know that: "The way you serve the vision is by developing people so that they can work on that vision even when you're not around ... that was the power of Jesus' leadership – the leaders he trained went on to change the world when he was no longer with them in bodily form."

Greenleaf (1977) used his conceptual talent to revolutionise the discipline of leadership, by promoting the concept of servant leadership. Today many years after his passing in 1990, Greenleaf's dream is alive and well. The paradigm of servant leadership is promoted globally. And on 21st and 22nd June 2012 the *2nd Global Servant Leadership Research Roundtable Conference* was held at Monash University Melbourne Australia and attended by leaders from countries around the world. Hence many years after the death of Greenleaf the servant leadership approach still 'inspires' contemporary leaders to be proactive and to engage in visionary leadership as they continue to move forward into the future with a strong sense of purpose (Greenleaf, 2002).

Foresight

Foresight is closely related to conceptualisation. Foresight is a necessary ingredient in the 'make-up' of an effective leader (Greenleaf, 1977). A leader, who has foresight, trusts and respects others and is intuitive. Such a leader realises that to be comfortable with the inner and the outer 'self' is to be comfortable with one's sense of 'self', and that this insight will follow through in one's relationship with others and result in a shared visioning process (Blanchard, 2007:229; cited in Cameron, 2009:32).

Greenleaf (2002:35) stresses that a leader "needs two intellectual abilities ... the leader needs to have *'a sense for the unknowable* and be able to *foresee the unforeseeable.*" Such a leader has intuition and is able to anticipate a problem/s before a potential situation gets out of hand. According to Greenleaf (1977:23), "The art of leadership rests, in part, on the ability to bridge that gap by intuition, that is, a judgment from the unconscious process." And again he stresses, "Foresight is the 'lead' that the leader has. Once leaders lose this lead and events start to force their hand, they are leaders in name only" (Greenleaf, 2002:40). Leadership in action requires leaders to anticipate and respond to problems before they escalate. Such a leader is intuitive and proactive seeking solutions to problems before they get out of hand.

Prophecy is linked to foresight. And in his early work Greenleaf (1977:221) refers to 'seekers' as "contemporary prophets" and quotes two very different 'prophets', the first – Jean Jaurès, a French Socialist leader who stated "Take from the altar of the past the fire, not the ashes" (1977:223), and the second – Matsuo Bashō, a Japanese poet, advised: "Do not seek to follow the footsteps of men of old. Seek what they sought" (ibid.). Greenleaf (cited in Fraker and Spears, 1996:38) likens a leader who has foresight to a leader having prophetic vision "The prophet ... is one who imagines what will later be proved."

According to Spears (1998:5), "Foresight is a characteristic that enables the servant leader to understand the lessons from the past, the realities of the present, and the likely consequences of a decision for the future. It is also deeply rooted in the intuitive mind." Interestingly in 1998 Spears noted the continuing lack of research into foresight as a focus for leadership studies and in 2010 again emphasised that "it is [still] a largely … unexplored area" (p. 25).

Stewardship

Peter Block (1993:xx) defines stewardship as "Holding something in trust for another." Michael McCuddy and Wendy Pirie (2007) maintain that "stewardship has both secular and spiritual implications." They interpret stewardship as "a mechanism of service to others … it clearly revolves around service to … [humankind]." This service involves looking after all resources human and non-human, "that God has entrusted to our care" and maintaining these resources to benefit all generations.

Stewardship is accepting responsibility and being accountable for decisions made. It promotes leaders as agents of change (McCuddy and Pirie, 2007; cited in Cameron, 2012:34). According to Sims (1997) leaders who value stewardship are custodians of nature and stewards of the sacredness of life. Rough (2011) maintains that "This characteristic [of stewardship] brings with it the weights of responsibility, perseverance, diligence, ownership and accountability."

To have a sense of stewardship is to have an awareness of the sense of connectedness that exists between the inner self and the world. In these changing times this type of leadership is being referred to as an ecology of leadership (Julie Boyd, 2012) where leaders are encouraged to have a global perspective whereby they reflect on the realities of the twenty-first century, taking into account "the challenges that transcend the complex systems within the natural environment" (ibid.) and develop an "awareness of the interconnectedness of all realities – spiritual, cosmic and existential" (Fritjof Capra, cited in Spears, 1998:119; cited in Cameron, 2012). Such a worldview requires contemporary leaders to change the way they think about leadership and management for according to Boyd (2012) this approach to leadership:

> emphasizes individual responsibility, partnership and interdependence, a long term perspective, flow cycles and capacities within organizations, understanding and implementing the principles of natural systems, diversity, co-evolution, harmony with nature, and leading the way toward sustainability for future generations.

Peter Senge (1996) maintains that leaders must create "an environment in which people are open to new ideas, responsive to change, and eager to develop new skills and capabilities." Being accountable and recognising the need for change to sustain viability in the future is what determines responsible stewardship and this value-driven approach doesn't just happen (cited in Cameron, 2014).

Hence leaders who are "stewards of the human and institutional resources entrusted to their care" (Stubbs, cited in Spears, 1998:316) will have a cosmic vision and engage in transformative action to mentor and nurture, to facilitate and utilise the talents and gifts of others by empowering them to be the best they can be in their service of stewardship to the global community (cited in Cameron, 2014).

Commitment to the growth of people

There are times in our lives when we are called upon to be leaders and times when we are called to be followers however whether we are called to be leaders or followers we are called to service. In sum we are all learners coming together at different levels of competency, creating knowledge and learning from one another. To commit to the growth of people is to value and respect their ethnicity and diversity without discrimination. And such a commitment enables leaders to engage in ethical practice with behaviour that is objective, responsible and accountable in an inclusive environment that promotes justice and fairness for all. Commitment to the growth of people is the essence of what servant leadership teaches, for according to Greenleaf the test is, "Do those served grow as persons? Do they, while being served, become healthier, wiser, freer more autonomous, more likely themselves to become servant" (Greenleaf, 1977:13-14; cited in Cameron, 2012:35).

Servant leaders nurture the human and spiritual growth of those they lead. They mentor and foster the talents and skills of others and empower them to be the best they can be (Greenleaf, 1977) for "Potential bearers of responsibility need special help to mature their talents just as athletes do" (1977:197). According to Rough (2011) members of a team need to feel they have a 'voice' and "if a member feels devalued, ignored, or powerless, then the organization will suffer and a culture will be created that greatly weakens the overall effectiveness ... [of the team and/or organization]."

A shared leadership approach encourages all members of a team to work together. Blanchard maintains:

> In high performing organizations power and decision making are shared and distributed throughout the organization not guarded at the top of the hierarchy. Participation, collaboration and team work are a way of life. When people feel valued and respected for their contributions, are allowed to make decisions that impact their lives, and have access to information to make good decisions they can and will

function as valuable contributors to the person and vision of the organization (2007:13).

In such an environment where each person motivates the other there is mutual respect. Hunter (2004:185) cites Bob Nelson, organisational manager, on the importance of motivation, "You get the best effort from others not by lighting a fire beneath them but by building a fire within them." Leaders need to inspire the members of their team and give them the opportunity to grow and whether the members of the organisation are leaders or followers they are all sharing and serving the same vision for the future.

Building community

When members of the team work together collaboratively they build a sense of community. Building community is about applying the principles of servant leadership to create "a healthy environment in which people can live and work free of unnecessary barriers and distractions ... Many great organizations possess this capacity to create an environment in which the differences – social, political, ethnic, positional, racial, and others – are transcended" (Hunter, 2004:207). Members of the team are then empowered and educated to reach their potential, their human and spiritual needs are nurtured. They are disciplined.

Jesus Christ, leader and builder of the Church community, "came to serve the vision that he had been given by His Father. He came as a teacher, as a leader, as a trainer to prepare people to go out and help other people live according to that vision" (Blanchard and Hodges, 2003:56-57). This inspiring of others can be accomplished by all members of a group or team being responsible for building the communities in their lives, and regardless of the roles they undertake – as leaders or followers, they are all 'team players' and they are here, at this time, and in this place, to make a difference (Blanchard and Hodges, 2003).

Sims (1997:68-70) refers to the influence of the spirit in building community and maintains that the spirit reconnects, "The human soul is reconnected to one's larger self, immersed and fulfilled in the experience of community ... the ... great work of the spirit is the building and restoring of community." Sims (1997:134) emphasises that everyone has a purpose and as members of the "human community, all need to work together for the good of all: 'There are no observers, only participants. Nobody is 'on' the earth as an object; every living entity is 'in' the earth as a subject – as part of a vast pulsating, interwoven web of life'" (cited in Cameron, 2012:39).

Leaders who are motivated will not be content with the 'status quo'. They will be creative in their efforts as change agents and in order to support the members of their team/s they will often step outside their comfort zone disregarding any perceived criticism that may emanate from outsiders for, "Those outside can criticise ... and disrupt, but only those who are inside can build. For the servant who has the capacity to be a builder, the greatest joy in the world is in building" (Greenleaf, 1977:248). And building community is about ensuring survival from one generation to the next.

Now the above list of ten core characteristics common to the servant leader is by no means exhaustive. For there are many characteristics and values that are just as valid as the ten core characteristics and these can be found in leaders who are most admired for their leadership skills and who may demonstrate some or all of the following character traits: charism, respect, love, integrity, kindness, gentleness, patience, joy and much, much more! So the potential then is for an unlimited number of character traits that may epitomise the make-up and practice of the servant leader (cited in Cameron, 2012).

In the chapters that comprise PART TWO a number of insights are revealed when the ten core characteristics of servant leadership are applied to the life and works of St Hildegard of Bingen.

PART TWO

THE TEN CORE CHARACTERISTICS OF
SERVANT LEADERSHIP APPLIED TO THE LIFE
AND WORKS OF HILDEGARD OF BINGEN

6

LISTENING

Hildegard possessed the skill of listening and this is demonstrated by her response to the 'inner voice' heard during the many visions she experienced. Listening to the inner voice is described by John Gardiner (cited in Spears, 1998:116), as being attuned to a "'quiet presence,' … [which is a place] 'where leadership and the Spirit meet.'" Spears (1998:4) maintains that it is only when listening to the 'inner voice' that a person recognises "what the body, spirit and mind are communicating." In the 'Declaration' to the *Scivias* Hildegard informs us that: "In the forty-third year of my earthly course, as I was gazing with great fear and trembling attention at a heavenly vision, I saw a great splendour in which resounded a voice from Heaven, saying to me. 'O fragile human, ashes of ashes … Say and write what you see and hear'" (cited in *Scivias*, 1990:59).

Hildegard listened to the dictates of the 'voice from Heaven' and as you may remember from Chapter 2 she had been experiencing visions from childhood, but it was this particular vision that was to change her life. For Hildegard began to question whether the 'voice' she heard was indeed of divine origin and she wondered if she should continue to listen – for how could she discern whether the voice was from God or if it was just an illusion? Self-doubt began to torment Hildegard. Pope Benedict XVI (2010a:1) writes that in her dilemma "She thus turned to a person who was most highly esteemed in the Church in those times: St Bernard of Clairvaux … [who] calmed and encouraged Hildegard."

Hildegard wrote to Bernard expressing her anxiety at receiving these visions for she wanted advice on how she should proceed:

> Father, I am greatly disturbed by a vision which had appeared to me through divine revelation, a vision seen not with my fleshly eyes but only in my spirit ... I have from earliest childhood seen great marvels which my tongue has no power to express but which the Spirit of God has taught me that I may believe ... Through this vision which touches my heart and soul like a burning flame, teaching me profundities of meaning. I have an inward understanding of the Psalter, the Gospels, and other volumes. Nevertheless I do not receive this knowledge in German. Indeed, I have no formal training at all, for I know how to read only on the most elementary level, certainly with no deep analysis. But please give me your opinion in this matter (cited in Joseph Baird, 2006:17-18).

Bernard replied to Hildegard's letter in a positive way and endorsed that her visions were indeed from God. Baird (2006:20) tells us that Bernard intervened on Hildegard's behalf with Pope Eugenius III who happened to be close by at Trier where the Bishops had assembled for a Synod (1147-1148). Hildegard had already commenced writing the *Scivias* but over the years she had remained quiet about her visions and recording their content, having probably only confided in those closest to her – Jutta and Volmar (whom we will see later became her secretary and close friend) and so Flanagan (1998:42) writes that Hildegard was reluctant up until now to speak up about what she had heard: "I was very fearful and ashamed to publish what I had kept silent for so long." Nevertheless Hildegard listened to the advice of Bernard of Clairvaux and as a result "While ... the [*Scivias*] was still in progress a portion was shown to Pope Eugenius III; ... [who read] from it to the prelates assembled at the Synod of Trier ... Eugenius gave papal approval both to this text and to whatever else Hildegard might produce by means of the Holy Spirit" (Flanagan, 1995:2). Upon learning that she had received official papal recognition for her work that was deemed 'divinely inspired' Hildegard became more confident and began to write and speak with authority.

Flanagan (1998:42) emphasises that when the 'voice' commanded Hildegard to "Say and write what you see and hear" Hildegard was in effect being asked to write down her visions and also to engage in preaching activities. However for the time being Hildegard opted to just write down what she had seen and heard "perhaps this was because while there were definite prohibitions against women preaching, the issue of their writing was less clear cut" (ibid.) and later in Chapter 11 when the characteristic *Conceptualisation* is discussed, more will be revealed regarding Hildegard's preaching activities in her mission of service to the Church.

Referring back to the *Scivias* and in addition to that written by Flanagan (1998), Carmen Butcher (2013:11) writes that "Letters suggest that Pope Eugenius may have read from the first two stunning visions of *Scivias'* second book. The text he read so impressed the assembly [at Trier] … that the Pope wrote to Hildegard, commanding her to keep on writing" and the response of Hildegard to these words of praise from the Pope is noted in a previous paragraph.

The visions of Hildegard were all seen with the 'inner eye' and heard with the 'inner ear' – she saw she listened and she responded! Hildegard asserted that all her visions were divinely inspired and were the result of inward revelation (*Scivias*, 1990:59-60). Such is reflective listening which is a skill that "enables the listener to understand the content of the message as well as the feelings of the person who is speaking" (DeGraaf et al., 2001:4). You may recall from Chapter 2 that it was from about the age of five that Hildegard had begun experiencing visions. And according to Silvas (1998:138) "as soon as she [Hildegard] was able to attempt her first words she would describe to those around her, both in words and gestures the shape of her hidden visions."

However Hildegard does not claim that the visions she experienced resulted from ecstasy. Also she emphasises that in relating the visions she is just repeating what she has heard. For Silvas (1998:114) notes "She [Hildegard] asserts that she does not see these visions in a sleeping state, but awake, so that in all this she never suffers the unconsciousness of ecstasy, and that in describing these visions she uses no other words than those she has heard."

Throughout the *Scivias* (1990), there are instances of Hildegard's listening to divine revelation. For example: "I heard a voice from Heaven saying to me, 'Cry out therefore, and write thus!'" (p. 61). As Hildegard recounts her visions (1990) she introduces many reflective comments commencing with words similar to the following "And again I heard the voice from Heaven, saying to me ..." (p. 94). "And again I heard the living Light, saying to me ..." (p. 161). Early on in the *Scivias* during 'Vision One on the Redeemer' Hildegard links the inner reality of listening to the voice of the 'living light':

> ... I heard the voice from on high saying to me, "You may not see anything further regarding this mystery unless it is granted you by a miracle of faith" ... And I heard the voice saying to me ... "O you who are wretched earth and, as a woman, untaught in all learning of earthly teachers and unable to read literature with philosophical understanding, you are nonetheless touched by My light, which kindles in you an inner fire like a burning sun; cry out and relate and write these My mysteries that you see and hear in mystical visions. So do not be timid, but say those things you understand in the Spirit as I speak them through you ..." (1990:150).

And so the *Scivias* is the first and perhaps best-known work of what is referred to as Hildegard's trilogy of works though Flanagan does emphasise that "Hildegard may not have envisaged them as such" (1995:3). The *Scivias* took ten years to write (1141-1151). In this work Hildegard sums up her visions – Benedict (2010b:2) refers to thirty-five visions though the number recorded in the *Scivias* itself (1990) is twenty-six. In his discussion of the *Scivias* Benedict informs us that Hildegard is describing "the events of the history of salvation from the creation of the world to the end of time. With the characteristic traits of feminine sensitivity [that is Hildegard is listening and taking note of her feminine side] Hildegard develops at the very heart of her work the theme of the mysterious marriage between God and humanity that is brought about in the Incarnation" (2010b:2). The *Scivias* comprises three books and each book refers to visions experienced by Hildegard with Book One referring to six visions; Book Two referring to seven visions and Book Three referring to thirteen visions – in total twenty-six visions (Hart and Bishop [Trans.], cited in *Scivias*, 1990:55).

The second 'visionary' work produced by Hildegard between 1158 and 1163 is *Liber Vitae Meritorum* (The Book of Life's Merits). Butcher (2013:135) notes that this book contains six visions that "focus on the temptations every Christian encounters and how God can help those who love Him resist these. Hildegard having listened to the 'divine directives' details thirty-five vices, plus their punishments and fitting acts of penance." Benedict (2010b:2) reviews this work of Hildegard saying "she describes a unique and powerful vision of God who gives life to the cosmos with his power and his light … the work is centred on the relationship between virtue and vice, which is why human beings must face the daily challenge of vice that distances them on their way towards God and of virtue that benefits them."

The final instalment of the trilogy is the *Book of Divine Works* which Butcher (2013:149) informs us also took Hildegard a decade to write "She was an old woman when she finished it in 1173 [which is the year of the death of her secretary, friend and confidant, the monk Volmar] – at seventy-five … [and] some call … [this work] her best, most mature visionary creation. It presents ten visions in three parts." Benedict (2010b:2) discusses Hildegard's efforts saying that this work is considered by many as her masterpiece where "she once again describes creation in its relationship with God and the centrality of the human being, expressing a strong Christo-centrism with a biblical-Patristic flavour."

Hildegard listened and responded with faith to the inner voice. Gardiner (cited in Spears, 1998:116) quotes Gandhi's insight, "faith is nothing but a living, wide-awake consciousness of God within." And Gardiner (cited in Spears, 1998:117; cited in Cameron, 2012) quotes Ralph Waldo Emerson's dictum, "The highest revelation is that God is in very man." Pope Benedict XVI (2010b:2) refers to Hildegard's ability to be attuned to her inner self and engage in reflective listening as she responds to her visions. He says that "In a letter to St Bernard the mystic from the Rhineland [Hildegard] confesses":

> The vision fascinates my whole being: I do not see with the eyes of the body but it appears to me in the spirit of the mysteries ... I recognize the deep meaning of what is expounded on in the Psalter, in the gospels and in other books, which have been shown to me in the vision. This vision burns like a flame in my breast and in my soul and teaches me to understand the text profoundly (Epistolarium pars prima I-XC: CCCM 91).

Carmel Posa (2012:2) refers to Hildegard as a "discerning Benedictine Abbess who listened with the ear of her heart and found her own authentic voice because of it. She models for us the listening Joan Chittister describes: *'Listen with a critical ear for the sound of the gospel in everything you do.'*"

According to Filippa Anzalone (2007:798) "To listen at a level that will build healthy relationships, the leader must be psychologically integrated and in touch with his or her own inner core ... To really hear, the listener looks beyond him or herself for the moment and presents an open mind, and heart, to the follower." By being in touch with her inner reality Hildegard not only produced her trilogy of works [and other compositions referred to in this chapter] but she composed a 'symphony of song'. Butcher (2013:23) maintains that "Hildegard's music is the most intimate glimpse she left us of her heart. It is passionate, fresh, inventive, bold, and layered with meaning." And "Hildegard took special pleasure in writing liturgical music to celebrate the heroic lives of saints. Three of her favorites were St. Disibod, St. Rupert, and St Ursula" (Butcher, 2013:28).

In reference to Hildegard's music Flanagan (1998:102) devotes a chapter entitled 'Celestial Harmonies' and maintains "While there is no debate about the authorship of the musical works, there is some question about when they were composed." For Degler tells us that the works could have been composed as early as 1141 or at any time during the years that followed even in "her later years":

> Regardless, by the end of her life Hildegard had composed over seventy songs that were eventually combined into a cycle she called the *Symphony of the Harmony of Celestial Revelations*. Today this music is sung and recorded around the world and celebrated for both the powerful, innovative use of melody and for the poetic beauty of the lyrics (2007:6).

Symphony of the Blessed is the final vision – (No. 13) in Hildegard's first major work the *Scivias* (1990:525). This 'Symphony' includes 'Songs to Holy Mary'; and songs – 'To the nine orders of heavenly spirits', 'To the patriarchs and prophets', 'To the apostles', 'To the martyrs', 'To the confessors', 'To the virgins', 'The lament over the ones to be recalled' and 'The exhortation of the virtues and the fight against the Devil' … Hildegard introduced this final section of her work as follows:

> *Then I saw the lucent sky in which I heard different kinds of music, marvellously embodying all the meanings I had heard before. I heard the praises of the joyous citizens of Heaven, steadfastly persevering in the ways of Truth; and laments calling people back to those praises and joys; and the exhortations of the virtues, spurring one another on to*

> *secure the salvation of the peoples ensnared by the Devil ... And their song, like the voice of a multitude, making music in harmony praising the ranks of Heaven* ... (cited in *Scivias*, 1990:525).

Listening to others and then taking time to listen to the inner voice, is a source of wisdom for the leader who then becomes conscious of the needs of followers and conscious of his or her own inner needs (Spears, 1998). Butcher notes Hildegard's letter to the 'Prelates of Mainz' expressing how music affects both the interior and the exterior reality of the soul:

> Music stirs our hearts and engages our souls in ways we can't describe. When this happens, we are taken beyond our earthly banishment back to the divine melody Adam knew when he sang with the angels, when he was whole in God, before his exile ... and if Adam had never lost the harmony God first gave him, the mortal fragilities that we all possess today could never have survived hearing the booming resonance of that original voice (cited in Butcher, 2013:125-126).

Benedict in his Apostolic Letter proclaiming Hildegard a *Doctor of the Universal Church* maintains that Hildegard listened to the Word of God as expressed in the Books of the Old and the New Testament:

> Precisely because God "speaks", man is called to listen. This concept affords Hildegard the opportunity to expound her doctrine on song, especially liturgical song. The sound of the word of God creates life and is expressed in his creatures. Thanks to the creative word, beings without rationality are also involved in the dynamism of creation. But man of course is the creature who can answer the voice of the Creator with his own voice. And this can happen in two ways: *in voce oris*, that is, in the celebration of the liturgy, and *in voce cordis*, that is through a virtuous and holy life. The whole of human life may therefore be interpreted as harmonic and symphonic (2012a:3).

People, who have the ability to hear, have the ability to listen. There are many theories on how best to listen. These theories revolve around active listening and reflective listening. Greenleaf (1977:300; cited in Cameron, 2012:17) defines listening as a skill whereby a person is receptive to what is said and not said. He quotes an old Italian proverb: "From listening comes wisdom." And so balancing body, mind and soul is an important strategy when implementing the servant leadership characteristic of listening.

The investigation into the remaining characteristics of servant leadership reveals many examples of Hildegard's listening skills. DeGraaf et al. (2001:3) have stated that listening is the first characteristic of servant-leaders, "for it is through listening that many of the other characteristics can be nurtured" (cited in Cameron, 2012:19).

7

Empathy

Empathy is "the ability to go deep into relationships" (Cliff Medney, 2008:1). To have empathy is to have an acceptance of others, recognising and building on their strengths and accepting their limitations, and not rejecting them (Greenleaf, 2002:33-34). According to DeGraaf et al. (2001:5) "Empathy is the capacity for participation in another's feelings or ideas … People need to be accepted and recognised for their special and unique spirits."

Hildegard's empathetic skills are evident through her concern and compassion for others particularly through her empathy and love for the Church, its members and her sisters in religion. In fact Hildegard empathised with most people with whom she came in contact. However in those early years at the monastery at Disibodenberg Silvas (1998:97) informs us that such contacts were few for her only source of companionship was Jutta von Sponheim (her spiritual mother) and one other (also referred to as Jutta) when they were living in the anchorhold (see Chapter 2).

Prior to Hildegard leaving home her parents had approached Jutta von Sponheim and "begged her earnestly to be so generous as to take to herself their daughter who they had set apart for holy celibacy and divine service, so that she might stay with her always." Jutta agreed and in time became Hildegard's spiritual mother – her *magistra*. The relationship was close. "For Jutta, having died to the world and withdrawn from it, was more fruitful in her one spiritual heir and daughter Hildegard, as can be seen today than if she had been given in marriage and had brought forth a greater number of offspring through generation of the flesh" (Silvas, 1998:108).

Little is known of these early years at the monastery though Hildegard "must have distinguished herself in some way … because when the Abbess Jutta died in 1136 Hildegard was unanimously chosen as her successor" (Degler, 2007:4-5). This vote of confidence shows that Hildegard empathised and related well with her sisters in religion … [for they had] chosen her "to exercise the supervision of discipline over them … for they were secure concerning her discernment and self-control" (Silvas, 1998:111).

It was around 1141 when Hildegard was "commanded … 'to say and write' what she 'saw and heard' in her visions" (ibid.) that she realised she needed a secretary – someone to whom she could relate her experiences who would listen to her and a relationship fostered where there would be mutual trust – for mutual trust is another aspect of empathy. Both leaders and followers need to respect each others' integrity and allow for the autonomy of the other (Greenleaf, cited in Fraker and Spears, 1996:54). Silvas (1998:116) writes that "there became known to her a monk [Volmar] in that same monastery who was sober, chaste and learned in the wisdom of both heart and word … exercising the restraint of his editorial work he clothed her words – however bare and unpolished – in a more presentable dress."

In other words Silvas adds that Hildegard either dictated what she wanted written down or wrote down the information and her scribe Volmar "rendered their cases, tenses, and conjugations according to the exactness of the grammatical art which she did not know, while he presumed neither to add nor subtract anything to their sense or meaning" (1998:155). The friendship between Hildegard and the 'priest-monk' Volmar was to last a lifetime. Volmar accompanied Hildegard and her nuns when they relocated to Rupertsberg (see Chapter 2) and he continued to minister to them with his spiritual guidance and secretarial skills until his death in 1173.

Newman (1990:12) tells us "After she overcame her initial hesitation about writing, it took Hildegard ten years to complete the *Scivias* with the editorial help of Volmar and the assistance and moral support of her favorite nun, Richardis von Stade." Hildegard had developed a deep affection – a form of motherly love for this young nun Richardis von Stade. Close friendships between nuns have never been encouraged in the convent (Cameron, 2012) though it appears as if the rapport between Hildegard and Richardis was more of a mother/daughter relationship.

Butcher (2013:12) notes that "One year after relocating her community to Rupertsberg … Hildegard finished dictating *Scivias* to Volmar, the prior of her new Rupertsberg community, and to the nun Richardis of Stade, her other close friend, whom she called her 'daughter'." You may recall that Hildegard and her group of about "twenty noble women of wealthy parents" (Silvas, 1998:164) had relocated to Rupertsberg around 1150 and then Hildegard concentrated on completing the *Scivias*. It was during this time that she expressed her innermost feelings for Richardis:

> For while I was writing the book *Scivias* I bore a deep love for a certain noble young woman, daughter of the … Marchioness … just as Paul loved Timothy. She joined herself to me in loving friendship in everything, and comforted me in all my trials, until at length I finished that book (cited in Silvas, 1998:165).

Hildegard completed writing the *Scivias* in 1151 and shortly afterwards Richardis was appointed Abbess of Bassum. Now empathy recognises the potential in others and empowers them in their mission of service. DeGraaf et al. (2001:5) refer to empathy as, "The capacity for participation in another's feelings or ideas." Empathy is "making a difference in the lives of people and bringing out their magnificence by assisting them to achieve their goals" (Blanchard, 2007:250).

However although Hildegard recognised the potential in Richardis she was reluctant to let her go; she wanted the young nun to serve and achieve her goals by remaining at Rupertsberg with her [Hildegard] as spiritual mother. Baird (2006:39) writes that Hildegard was devastated by the thought of Richardis' departure and she felt that she needed to act for she believed that such a move was "out of concordance with God's eternal plan." Hence:

> [Hildegard] swung into action immediately, firing off missive after missive, alternately pleading, wheedling, threatening, stubbornly refusing to the end to give in to the inevitable. Letters poured out ... to the mother, to the brother, to the archbishop who had ordered her to comply, and ultimately, to the pope himself (Baird, 2006:40).

Hildegard sincerely believed that she knew what was best for her young charge as is evidenced from excerpts from her letters. In a Letter to the Margravine Richardis von Stade, regarding her daughter Richardis and granddaughter Adelheid (each had received an appointment as an abbess): "… I beseech and urge you not to trouble my soul so grievously that you make me weep bitter tears … the position of abbess that you desire for them is certainly, certainly, certainly not God's will, nor compatible with the salvation of their souls …" (Hildegard, cited in Baird, 2006:41).

Hildegard and the Margravine had been quite close until this encounter for the latter had been very supportive of the move of Hildegard and her group of nuns from Disibodenberg to Rupertsberg however in this letter she beseeches the mother to intercede and encourage Richardis to stay where she is loved and protected. However Hildegard received a letter from Heinrich Archbishop of Mainz who while acknowledging that "we have heard of your many wonderful miracles" (Baird, 2006:41) commanded that Hildegard release Richardis. The Archbishop then announced he would continue with his demands until they were obeyed. In return he receives a missive from Hildegard that is quite strongly worded:

> The Spirit of God says earnestly: "O Shepherds, wail and mourn over the present time, because you do not know what you are doing when you sweep aside the duties established by God in favor of opportunities for money and the foolishness of wicked men who do not fear God." And so your malicious cursed and threatening words are not to be obeyed. You have raised up your rods of punishment arrogantly, not to serve God, but to gratify your own perverted will (cited in Baird, 2006:42-43).

Baird (2006:42) emphasises that Hildegard believes she is "*Speaking through the voice of the Living Light … and supported by that divine authority, she utterly rejects his command. Indeed, she goes on the offense and accuses him of the sin of simony, the sale of Church offices for monetary gain.*" Hildegard also writes to Hartwig Archbishop of Bremen who is the brother of Richardis for she [Richardis] has been appointed Abbess at the monastery in Bassum which is in Hartwig's diocese and Hildegard knows that "he would indeed have the authority to return her" (cited in Baird, 2006:44). However Hartwig chooses to stand by the decision to have his sister appointed Abbess of Bassum.

Having met with resistance from many of the senior ecclesial administrators and with few options remaining Hildegard finally resorts to sending a letter to Pope Eugenius III in an effort to have her voice heard and her request approved. Baird (2006:45) states that the Pope leaves the decision up to the Archbishop of Mainz whom as you may remember has already informed Hildegard of his intentions and was therefore unlikely to change his mind.

> We rejoice, my daughter, and we exult in the Lord, because your honourable reputation has spread so far and wide that many people regard you as "the odour of life unto life" … we have delegated that matter you wished to consult us

about to our brother Heinrich, archbishop of Mainz (Pope Eugenius III, cited in Baird, 2006:46).

Hunter (2004:101) recommends that the servant "leader must develop the skill of letting go of the resentment that often lingers when people hurt us or let us down." Lamentably within twelve months of becoming Abbess of Bassum Richardis dies at the relatively young age of 28 (or thereabouts) and Hildegard is informed of the passing of her protégée by Hartwig. Despite her inexplicable feelings of grief Hildegard rallies and over time concentrates on ensuring the well-being of the sisters in her community. For as mentioned in Chapter Two the nuns are from noble families and many found the move from Disibodenberg to Rupertsberg quite difficult. However, regardless, they had all opted to follow Hildegard: "And although there was some disaffection among them, almost all of them stood by Hildegard through a period of severe adversity that lasted a full eight years" (Degler, 2007:9).

Degler (2007:9) reveals some of the emotional 'make-up' of this saint of Bingen: "Hildegard was not only compassionate, she was also a virtual firebrand when it came to issues of what we would call today social justice. She literally railed – with no concern for her own safety or well-being – against anyone she believed was unethical. To this end she wrote letters to kings, princes, bishops, and the Pope alike deploring the dissolution and corruption she saw around her."

Hildegard had a great love and concern for the Church and its members. Newman (1990:10) posits that "to her contemporaries Hildegard was 'the Sibyl of the Rhine', an oracle they sought out for advice on everything from marital problems and health troubles to the ultimate fate of their souls." And so Hildegard's correspondence was prolific and "Her many letters indicate the range of her influence, from high to low estates. She wrote to kings, queens and popes, archbishops, abbesses and abbots, nuns and monks, laywomen and laymen, seeking advice and giving it, even when it was not sought"

(Posa, 2012:1). And she did not hesitate in chastising people of 'note' – kings, bishops, priests, and all whom she considered preferred to satisfy their own needs at the expense of others – profiteers in a sense who were unethical and self-serving.

For example Degler (2007:8) writes of Hildegard's confrontation with the Emperor Frederick I (Barbarossa) who "when he came into power, granted Hildegard an edict of imperial protection from the battles and fighting that plagued the land during his reign." Because of this edict Hildegard and her nuns were guaranteed safety in their convent at Rupertsberg – which was a "considerable distance from the security of the monastery at Disibodenberg." Despite this show of generosity and having received the edict were not enough to stop Hildegard from admonishing Frederick for his actions in battle. Degler (ibid.) quotes Newman's account of a letter written by Hildegard to Frederick where she "'compares him to an infant and a madman' and in another repeats the words of God that have come to her: 'Woe, woe to the malice of wicked men who defy me! Hear this, king, if you wish to live; otherwise my sword shall smite you.' Fortunately for Hildegard, Frederick did not lift his edict of protection" in retaliation.

Newman (1990:10) maintains that Hildegard also "rebuked [Frederick] fiercely for his role in the German papal schism." Now this schism commenced in 1159 and is described by Baird as occurring when two rival popes were elected following the death of Pope Hadrian IV, "Alexander III and Victor IV. Frederick Barbarossa gave his approval to the latter, and when Victor died in 1164, Frederick, in blatant defiance of the Church elected his own pope, Paschal II, and, after him, another, Calixtus III. The schism lasted until 1177, when Frederick and Alexander III were reconciled" (2006:116).

Living during this era Hildegard had firsthand knowledge and experience of the consequences of the schism for the wellbeing and survival of the Church. And so it was that her empathetic nature led to her continuing concern for the Church and the clergy. However

Flanagan (1995:10) maintains that it was "the failure of the clergy to lead exemplary lives and to teach the people" that was linked with the rise of heretical sects and that the most prominent of these at the time being the Cathars who: "viewed the world and all its activities, especially procreation, as the Devil's work. [And] Catharism, which had spread from Bulgaria to the Rhineland by the middle of the twelfth century, was particularly active in Cologne" (Flanagan, 1998:63). Hildegard urged the clergy of Cologne to preach against Cathars in the city.

Pope Benedict XVI (2010b:3) praises Hildegard's influence in this regard "In a special way Hildegard countered the movement of German Cátari (Cathars). They Cátari means literally 'pure' advocated a radical reform of the Church, especially to combat the abuses of the clergy. She harshly reprimanded them for seeking to subvert the very nature of the Church." The clergy were also subject to reproach from Hildegard if found wanting in their duty to the Church. Degler (2007:10) quotes Newman's recount of a letter from Hildegard criticising some monks of the Cistercian Order. Apparently the "monks … had found the courage to ask her 'what in us and our order is displeasing to you, or rather to the eyes of God?'" Hildegard, says Newman, answers them by alluding to a "plethora of faults, notably presumption, instability, hypocrisy, and schism." The letter itself begins with the words, "'O sons of Israel, why have you corrupted tender Love', and goes on to use terms that range from 'audacious' to 'wicked' to refer to the order" (ibid.).

Hildegard's love and concern for the Church led to her undertaking preaching tours during her twilight years. Baird (2006:106) refers to her third preaching tour "*sometime between 1161 and 1163 (when she was in her mid-sixties).*" Baird maintains that "*Hildegard preached a fiery sermon to the clerics in the cathedral city of Cologne*" and that the dean and clerics of the cathedral sent a personal plea to Hildegard to: "*put down in writing the words that they had received only orally at that time, for they hold her words …*

to be 'from the very oracle of God.' What greater acclaim could Hildegard have achieved: a woman preaching to a male audience, castigating them, in no uncertain terms, for their sins – and making them like it?" (ibid.) Hildegard's sermon to the clerics at Cologne included the following:

> O my children, you who feed my flocks as the Lord commanded … you walk in filth like disgusting beasts … You do whatever your flesh demands … Through the teaching of the Scriptures, which were composed through the fire of the Holy Spirit, you ought to be the corners of the Church's strength, holding her up like the corners that sustain the boundaries of the earth. But you are laid low and do not hold up the Church, retreating instead to the cave of your own desire (cited in Baird, 2006:109-111).

Hildegard is rebuking the clerics for their behaviour and she believes that God is speaking through her when she tells his clerics that they are selfish and self-serving. Greenleaf (2002:33-34) maintains that "The servant as leader always empathizes, always accepts the person but sometimes refuses to accept some of the person's effort or performance as good enough." Benedict (2010b:3) maintains that the clergy responded positively to the words of reprimand from Hildegard for "They all listened willingly, even when she spoke severely: they considered her a messenger sent by God. She called above all the monastic communities and the clergy to a life in conformity with their vocation." And interestingly the clerics did not seem to resent Hildegard's words of rebuke it was as if they sensed God's presence within her.

Degler (2007:8) refers to this innate presence as charisma and states that it was 'awakened' in Hildegard. And though Hildegard herself being a product of twelfth century Germany would not have even been aware of such a term, charisma is a gift which Degler (ibid.) emphasises can be attributed to her for charism can lead to "magnetism … [it can be] 'mind-alluring' … [and] worshiped even by kings." Clearly, from what we have seen in this section Hildegard had such an empathetic effect on people that any criticism by her seemed to be tolerated. For example "the Emperor Frederick put up with a diatribe from her that would have gotten most people beheaded [see previous paragraphs in this chapter]; she attracted large crowds when she spoke outside the convent, and many young women of noble birth were drawn to the convent because of her" (Degler, 2007:8). Such a leader inspires trust "the willingness of followers to be influenced by the charismatic leader is in part based upon their trust in the leader" (Kouzes and Posner, 1987; Yukl, 1989, cited in Jay Conger et al., 2000:750).

There are many more instances of Hildegard's empathetic responses to various people and situations during her lifetime but there is a limit to what can be recorded in this book on her life and works. However an incident that Hildegard experienced towards the end of her long life is a testament to her compassion, love, tolerance and passion for justice and for equity for another human being. When Hildegard was eighty years of age (remember she died at the age of eighty-one) she was ordered by representatives speaking for the Archbishop of Mainz to remove the body of a nobleman (whose name is unknown) who had been buried in the consecrated convent grounds at Rupertsberg.

> [The prelates of] Mainz claimed that the man had died excommunicate and therefore had not been entitled to burial in consecrated ground. Hildegard politely refused, replying that to her own knowledge the man had been absolved and had been reconciled with the church before death and to remove him from sacred ground would be a terrible sin (Degler, 2007:10).

Hildegard refused to exhume the body arguing that the man had indeed been previously excommunicated from the Church but that he had *"been fully reconciled to the Church before his death"* (Baird, 2006:155). Hildegard and her nuns even went so far as to remove the headstones and disguise the grave so that it would not be easily found if the Archbishop's representatives came to the convent to force an exhumation of the body. The demands from Mainz persisted and before long a harsh penalty was imposed on Hildegard and her nuns and all in the convent were placed under an ecclesiastical interdict. The terms of the interdict were stringent: "they were forbidden to partake of Mass [that is forbidden reception of the Eucharist] and they could only perform the Holy Offices – the prayers that they were accustomed to recite for literally hours every day – in a subdued form behind closed doors. They were also forbidden to use any liturgical music" (Degler, 2007:10). It was only about six months prior to the death of Hildegard that the interdict was lifted when she was proven to be correct in her version of events which was corroborated by witnesses – for the nobleman had indeed received absolution prior to his death.

Hildegard had not condoned the actions of the nobleman nor did she condemn him in death for decisions made during his lifetime. She was fighting for justice and for what she believed was right regardless of the consequences. Blanchard (2007:xxii) states "your treatment of people is leadership in action." Hildegard had accepted that the man was a sinner but a sinner who had shown remorse and who had asked forgiveness for his behaviour. Greenleaf (2002:34) writes of the importance of acceptance "Acceptance of the person … requires a tolerance of imperfection." So a servant leader accepts the humanity of a person whoever they are and whatever they have done and empathises with them – this is what Hildegard did and as we have seen at great spiritual and physical cost to her sisters and herself.

8

HEALING

Healing in servant leadership is concerned with the spiritual, psychological and physical dimensions of the human composition in other words, with the complicated structure that is the 'whole' human person (Spears, 1998). DeGraaf et al. (2001:7) maintain that healing addresses "the spiritual side of leadership ... [and that healing] is a powerful force for transformation and integration." Greenleaf writes about this transformational aspect of servant leadership "[t]here is something subtle communicated to one who is being served and led if, implicit in the compact between the servant-leader and led is the understanding that the search for wholeness is something that they have" (1991, cited in Anzalone, 2007:799).

As is evidenced in this chapter Hildegard's healing skills were highly developed. Silvas (1998:184) quotes from the *Third Book on the Miracles of Saint Hildegard* which emphasises that "SO POWERFUL A CHARISM of healings shone out in the blessed virgin, that scarcely anyone approached her sick who did not immediately regain good health." Posa (2012:1) tells us that Hildegard was "versed in medicine." And as mentioned in Chapter 4 Hildegard authored works on medicine and natural sciences. Specifically she wrote on medicine and nature (natural philosophy and medicine) in the *Physica* and *Causae et Curae* which became her "Classic Works on Health and Healing" (Throop, 1998). According to Silvas:

> The prodigious genius of Hildegard poured itself out in the second half of her life in a flurry of literary works ... She

was well known as a wonder-worker, and there are many interesting tales of her healings in her *Vita* [the story of her life] and the *Acta Inquisitionis* [a document highlighting information in readiness for the canonisation of Hildegard], precious vignettes [portrayals] into the social life of the times. She had a special gift for dispelling demons and curing mental illnesses (2012:10).

You may recall from Chapter 4 that Hildegard made "no claim to divine inspiration" (Newman, 1990:14) with her scientific works unlike her visionary writings for she "made a sharp distinction between God's work and her own." Newman further suggests that with "A tradition of miraculous healings ascribed to her … [Hildegard] practiced medicine informally, like many monastics; [and that] on the evidence of these writings, she used both natural and supernatural means" (ibid.).

Hildegard's *Physica*, and *Causae et Curae* are said to have been produced during the years 1151-1158 following the completion of *Scivias* 1151. In the *Physica* "Hildegard presents nine 'books' of healing systems: Plants, Elements, Trees, Stones, Fish, Birds, Animals, Reptiles, and Metals. In each book she discusses the qualities of these natural creations and elaborates on their medicinal use explaining how to prepare and apply different remedies" (Throop, 1998). Degler (2007:6) emphasises the importance placed on Hildegard's medical works by Dr Charles Singer who "In his classic work *From Magic to Science* in 1958 … gives Hildegard a pivotal place in the history of science. He states that her writings on cosmology "are heralds of the dawn of a new movement" and says that "with her we have left the Dark Ages and the Dawn (of Science) has begun." Degler (2007:6) does note however that "although most scholars accept Hildegard's authorship of these two medical texts, not all do."

Regarding *Causae et Curae* Throop is of the opinion that the work may be just an updated version of the *Physica* for "Much of it correlates word for word with the material in *Physica,* leading me to wonder if it may have been compiled at a later time" (1998:2). Flanagan describes both works with her description of the *Physica* similar to that of Throop. She describes the *Causae et Curae* stating that the title refers to five books "of varying lengths. It proceeds from cosmology and cosmography to the place of humanity in the world. There follows a version of traditional humoral theory ... which leads to a list of more than two hundred diseases or conditions to which humans are subject" (1995:5). Both works emphasise Hildegard's propensity for natural healing.

In her introduction to PHYSICA AND CAUSES AND CURES, Butcher (2013:127) states that:

> HILDEGARD'S COSMOLOGY and physiology are based on the four-humor, four-element approach dating back to the ancient Greeks. She believed a person's health depended on the balance of the four basic fluids, the 'humors' of blood, yellow bile, phlegm and black bile ... Because Hildegard saw the human body as a microcosm of the universe, she saw that these four humors were echoed in the four elements of air, fire, water, and earth.

Flanagan (1998:93) expands on this concept when she says that "Illnesses were thought to arise from an acute imbalance of these four humours [please note difference in spelling from above quotation], while certain characteristic types of personality (the choleric, sanguine, phlegmatic, and melancholic) were thought to be attributable to a chronic, constitutional imbalance of the humours." The human body consists of male and female. And Hildegard valued both male and female for she was cognizant of the emotional, spiritual, intellectual, psychological, and physical health of not just herself but others. Her search and thirst for knowledge seemed to know no bounds and as you read this chapter you will find there were few areas 'taboo' for this saint of Bingen who was equipped with an almost 'encyclopedic' knowledge of medical science while reaching out to all with her healing power. Throop (1998:2) writes that "Renown for her healing ability overwhelmed appreciation for her many other talents during her lifetime, and all ranks of people visited her for healing, exorcism, and counsel."

In her medical works Hildegard wrote about human sexuality and Flanagan maintains that "it is difficult to tell how much of her knowledge comes from experience or observation" and how much emanates from other influences for example external agencies or from her discussions with and treatment of 'patients' and/or from her experience as a "confidante and adviser to laywomen."

> Hildegard usually writes as if sexual intercourse takes place between husband and wife for the purpose of procreation … other forms of sexual expression and behaviour are recognized, usually without either commendation or condemnation. She has several different accounts of what determines the characteristics of the offspring conceived in different circumstances. In one instance she writes as if the sex of the child depends upon the strength of the man's semen (strong semen produces boys, weak semen girls), while the disposition of the child depends upon the amount of love the man and woman bring to the transaction (Flanagan, 1998:95).

Hildegard was of the opinion that conception depended upon the various phases of the moon and in her book Flanagan treats Hildegard's notion of this 'lunar effect' in greater detail though argues that "although it may have been possible to note the state of the moon on the day a child was born (and indeed most *lunaria* take this as the important time), there would have been great practical difficulties in determining the state of the moon at the child's conception" (1998:96).

Hildegard also goes into detail about men and women's sexual desires and uses metaphors and 'direct language' to get her message across (ibid.). In the fourth vision of the Book of Divine Works which is the final in her trilogy of works Hildegard writes that:

> Mankind is the culmination of divine handiwork … but the first man lacked a helper who was like him and so God gave him this helper who was his mirror image: woman. In her lay hidden the whole human race, which would be brought forth by the strength that had created the first man. Man and woman are therefore joined so that they can work together, for man without woman would not be known as such, likewise the woman. Woman is the work of man and man the instrument of feminine consolation, and neither can live separated from the other. Man shows forth the divinity; while woman manifests the humanity, of the Son of God … they have dominion over all creatures (cited in Wendy Brennan, 2003:20).

Flanagan maintains that "Hildegard's account of the place of sex in the earthly realm is, on the whole, remarkably optimistic … [and she] does describe in some explicit detail the nature of the sexual act 'from a woman's point of view'":

> When a woman is making love with a man, a sense of heat in her brain, which brings with it sensual delight, communicates the taste of that delight during the act and summons forth the emission of the man's seed. And when the seed has fallen into its place, that vehement heat descending from her brain draws the seed to itself and holds it, and soon the woman's sexual organs contract, and all the parts that are ready to open up during the time of menstruation now close, in the same way as a strong man can hold something enclosed in his fist (Peter Dronke, 1984:175-176, cited in Flanagan, 1998:97).

Hildegard is quite descriptive of her references to human sexuality and Flanagan (1998:95-98) posits that "What Hildegard has to say about women in general and their relationship to men is an important indicator of how she viewed her own capacities and capabilities." Flanagan refers to "some enduring sexual prejudices or stereotypes [in Hildegard's writing]: that men have uncontrollable urges but women do not; that men are ruled by their sexual appetites and women by their wombs, and the thwarting of either leads to trouble" (ibid.). The summation of her theories is that "the sexual relationship between men and women is unequal ... [for] Behind her theories ... is the basic notion that woman is weaker than man, because he was made from earth, and she from flesh" (Flanagan, 1998:98).

Hildegard also advised and counselled men and women of various sexual orientation and references to this can be found in the *Scivias*.

> God will judge all perpetrators of fornication, sodomy and bestiality ... [for] A man who sins with another man as if with a woman sins bitterly against God and against the union with which God united male and female ... And a woman who takes up devilish ways and plays a male role in coupling with another woman is most vile in My sight, and so is she who subjects herself to such a one in this evil deed ... God united man and woman, thus joining the strong to the weak, that each might sustain the other (cited in *Scivias*, 1990:278-279).

As a remedy for this and other forms of 'self-indulging sexual behaviour' Hildegard recommends 'certain penitential remedies' that include fasting and other forms of ascetical practices and also "Dietary measures as a preventative against excessive libidinousness [excessive sexual drive] ... in line with her medical views" (Flanagan, 1998:67). Hence while not condoning practices and behaviours which are contrary to the teachings of the Church Hildegard was inclusive in recommending treatment on how to approach such behaviour that could affect both males and females.

Hildegard wanted to relieve suffering. Her medicinal skills resulted in her being recognised as a healer – a physician. Degler elaborates:

> Hildegard ... took the time [from her busy schedule] to respond to the copious letters she received from nobles and commoners alike, seeking painstakingly in each response to communicate something that would help ease the person's suffering. And although she cared about all people regardless of gender, she seems to have been especially touched by the anguish of women. Much of the material in *Causes and Cures* ... deals with menstruation, conception, pregnancy, childbirth, and other women's issues. As Barbara Newman points out, although Hildegard cared deeply about the health of men, her, "...medical works and her reputed miracles reveal a solicitude for all the afflictions of women – in physical and mental illness, in barrenness and childbirth, in the throes of passion and the trials of marriage" (2007:9).

Though she lived until the age of eighty-one Hildegard suffered continually from ill health and indeed on many occasions her suffering was so excruciating that her sisters in religion prepared for the worst, as her illness at the time appeared to be life-threatening. Degler in her notes refers to the findings of some scholars and historians in regard to Hildegard's general health:

> *It is generally accepted that Hildegard suffered from, among other things, severely debilitating migraines. It needs to be noted that some scholars and historians, including Charles Singer, have made much of this fact and have proposed that her visions were nothing more than the distortions of perception and the flashing lights often associated with this type of headache* (2007:5).

You may recall from the introductory paragraphs in Chapter 2 that from childhood Hildegard was very fragile and suffered from chronic ill-health throughout her life. It was during those early years that she also first experienced the visions that would occur with increasing frequency as she grew into adulthood. Newman (1990:11) maintains that the link between the ill-health and the visions "strongly suggest a physiological basis. Charles Singer (see previous quotation) and more recently, Oliver Sacks have concluded that the abbess suffered from 'scintillating scotoma,' a form of migraine."

Newman emphasises that Hildegard did not try to "induce the visions" (1990:12). For she did not engage in severe ascetical practices – for example fasting and/or scourging her flesh. Caroline Walker Bynum (1987:26) writes about the medieval hagiographers and describes such behaviour as being common to the times when "women's devotion was more characterised by penitential asceticism, particularly self-inflicted suffering." Bynum in her Preface to the *Scivias* (1990:2) adds that being "A Benedictine Abbess, Hildegard advocated a monastic life of obedience and communal prayer – not the extravagant and individualistic asceticism of some later medieval women."

Newman (1990:12) reminds us that Hildegard was a Benedictine and as such "she practiced and counselled only moderate fasting and avoided mortifications; nor is it reported that she spent long hours in private prayer. Her visionary experience, then, was one of the givens of her physical and psychological make-up." Hildegard recounts an occasion when her health was of extreme concern:

> AT ONE TIME GOD laid me low on a bed of illness, and allowed excruciating airs to course through my whole body. The blood in my veins, the fluid in my body, even the marrow in my bones dried up so much it was as if my soul must be released from the body. I remained in that strife for thirty days such that my abdomen burned with the heat of a fiery air ... Even the strength of my spirit implanted in my flesh gave way, and though I did not pass out of this life, I was not fully in it either. My inert body was laid out over a haircloth on the ground, but my end was not yet in sight, though my superiors, my daughters and my neighbours came in great mourning to watch my passing (cited in Silvas, 1998:169).

DeGraaf et al. (2001:7) maintain that healing addresses "the spiritual side of leadership … [and that healing] is a powerful force for transformation and integration." Hildegard's gift was healing the body and spirit. Sims (1997:87) contends that very few leaders are called upon to heal as Jesus did, but he believes that leaders can model their leadership practices on other areas of Jesus' ministry (cited in Cameron, 2012). Sims explains: "Jesus' compassion was his constancy in reaching out at great personal cost to the despised and marginalized."

Hildegard followed in the footsteps of her master in her efforts to reach out to the sick, the poor and the marginalised. For example there are many miracles attributed to this saint of Bingen. Silvas (1998) recounts a number of Hildegard's 'healing' miracles in what is referred to as "THE THIRD BOOK ON THE MIRACLES OF THE HOLY VIRGIN HILDEGARD" (p. 210). A few examples are listed below:

> SO POWERFUL A CHARISM of healings shone out in the blessed virgin, that scarcely anyone approached her sick who did not immediately regain good health … (p. 184).
>
> … there was a domestic, Bertha, who used to serve the sisters faithfully. But a tumour on her neck and chest began to choke her aggressively. The affliction had so far advanced, that she could neither take food nor drink, nor even swallow her saliva. When she was brought to the servant of God, she begged with signs rather than words a remedy for the disease which was already well-nigh fatal. Feeling compassion for her, especially in view of her unstinting good service to them, she [Hildegard] traced the sign of the holy cross over the affected parts and restored her to the best of health (p. 185).
>
> IN BINGEN, THE DAUGHTER of a woman called Hazecha fell ill, and for three days was unable to speak. When her mother ran and sought the help of the holy virgin

for her daughter, she received from her only blessed water. But when her daughter sipped some of it, she immediately recovered her voice and her strength (p. 186).

Silvas (1998:187) writes that "whenever a small portion of her hair or clothing was applied to any of the sick, they were restored to their former health." Silvas cites examples where a plait from the hair of Hildegard was placed around the bodies of women suffering problems with childbirth and they subsequently delivered healthy babies.

> ON ANOTHER OCCASION THERE was a man who used to suffer acute attacks of epilepsy. In his anxiety he implored the venerable virgin to come to his aid. She made the sign of the Cross over him with a healing blessing and from that day forward he was never burdened with this affliction again. When he announced back at home that a miracle had been worked in him, many hastened to her for a remedy of the same affliction, and when she blessed them with the sign of the cross, they were set free (p. 192).

Even her death did not seem to hinder Hildegard from reaching out to relieve the pain and suffering of others. For according to Silvas (1998:210): "Marvellous indications of her merits were not lacking before she was buried. For two men, who, with fervent hope, made bold to touch her holy body, recovered from a severe illness. Her funeral rites were reverently celebrated by venerable men, and in a venerable place she was interred."

As mentioned at the beginning of this chapter Hildegard was blessed with a 'charism of healing' and Silvas refers to this 'charism' when she quotes from the *Book on Miracles of Saint Hildegard*: "AMONG OTHER SIGNS of her virtues, the Lord gave the holy virgin a charism of casting out demons from the bodies of the obsessed" (1998:184). Hildegard did not just heal the sick in body she also healed the sick in spirit. For example Baird (2006:80) notes:

> *In the year 1169, or thereabouts, Gedolphus, abbot of Brauweiler, wrote a letter to Hildegard, a woman he knew only by reputation. He wrote in despair, for he had on his hands a woman possessed of a devil, and despite all his efforts for some three long months, he had been unable to liberate her. At last, however, the devil himself had cried out that he could be cast out only by ... "the strength of your* [that is Hildegard's] *contemplation and the magnitude of divine revelation."*

Hildegard received the letter when she was on her sick bed but she responded with a letter to the Abbot informing him first of all of the differences regarding various 'evil spirits' and that it depends on these differences how they should be treated. "The demon you are inquiring about has those powers which resemble moral vices of human beings. For this reason, he gladly dwells among people and is not bothered by the Lord's cross, the relics of saints, or all the other things pertaining to service of God. Rather he mocks them, and stands in no awe of them" (Hildegard, cited in Baird, 2006:81). Hildegard sends her instructions on how the demon is to be 'cast out'. There is success for a time but unfortunately the demon reappears and is not vanquished until Hildegard herself administers the healing remedy.

Greenleaf (1977:227) maintains "Servant leaders are healers in the sense of making whole by helping others to a larger and nobler vision and purpose than they would be likely to attain for themselves." Hildegard's power of healing reflects this view. Throop (1998:6) asserts:

> Moderation is Hildegard's key to good health. In a letter to Elisabeth of Schönau, another Benedictine visionary, she advises the use of discretion, "Do not lay on more strain than the body can endure. Immoderate straining and abstinence bring nothing useful to the soul." Hildegard von Bingen advocated a balanced diet, sufficient rest, alleviation of stress, and a wholesome moral life.

This would have been wise advice for Hildegard's followers in the twelfth century and is still relevant in the twenty-first century for leaders who aspire to 'heal' – make whole – themselves and those they serve, for "Healing Leadership has meaning on at least two levels: restoring our leaders by bringing them back to emotional, spiritual, intellectual and physical health; and from the wisdom and insight gained through that healing process to provide, in turn, leadership that heals and transforms the quality of life and work [of the individuals and teams] within our organizations" (Judith Sturnick, cited in Spears, 1998:189).

Hildegard's motivation as a healer is in response to her own healing experiences encountered in this chapter. It would seem that Hildegard transformed the lives of others in light of knowledge gained through the numerous illnesses she suffered throughout her life. In Chapter 5 on the terms of reference for the ten core characteristics in the discussion on *Healing* there is reference to "the wounded Healer" which is a person who has experienced suffering, pain and healing and whose healing is then motivated by the desire to heal others (Daneault, 2008:1219). You may recall that Greenleaf states that healers are motivated by the desire to heal themselves while Spears (1998:4) writes of the power of healing, and that it is, "essential before transformation and wholeness can occur."

9

AWARENESS

According to Spears (2010:27) "General awareness, and especially self-awareness, strengthens the servant-leader. Awareness helps one in understanding issues involving ethics, power, and values. It lends itself to being able to view most situations from a more integrated, holistic position." Anzalone (2007:800) posits that "Awareness leads to self-knowledge and emotional maturity for both the servant leader and followers."

Hildegard's capacity for awareness was cultivated through her intuitive insight, knowledge of the spirituality of her times, visionary experiences and through general, spiritual and self-awareness. Greenleaf (1977:254) writes about spiritual awareness as a spiritual awakening, "[of] profound meaning for me, was the ... belief that the highest level of religious experience is awareness of oneness with the mystery ... the feeling of awe and wonder and amazement" (cited in Cameron, 2012). Remember in Chapter 2 that Hildegard experienced visions from early childhood but there was one visionary experience that changed her life forever. Hildegard experienced this spiritual awakening in 1141 some five years after her election as prioress in 1136:

> When I was forty-two years and seven months old, heaven was opened and a fiery light of exceeding brilliance came and permeated my whole brain, and inflamed my whole heart and my whole breast, not like a burning but a warming flame, as the sun warms anything its rays touch. And immediately I

knew the meaning of the exposition of the Scriptures, namely the Psalter, the Gospel and other catholic volumes of both the Old and the New Testaments (cited in the Introduction to the *Scivias*, 1990:59).

Upon experiencing this vision Hildegard refers to the fact that she then became aware of "the power and mystery of secret and admirable visions" (*Scivias*, 1990:60) that she had experienced since the "age of five" (ibid). Degler (2007:4) stresses that Hildegard now experienced awareness – and understood the texts "in spite of the fact that she did not previously know how to interpret the words of the Latin texts, to understand the grammar, or to even know how the syllables of the words were divided."

You may recall in Chapter 5 during the discussion on the terms of reference for the ten core characteristics when the characteristic *Awareness* was discussed that there was reference by Degler (2007) to – mystical experiences and/or enlightenment – being referred to as "the awakening of kundalini" which is defined in that chapter as "an evolutionary energy/consciousness force…" Therefore in reference to Hildegard's visionary 'encounter':

> This type of transformation in the level of understanding – accompanied by an overwhelming vision of light – is frequently alluded to in the writings on the awakening of kundalini … [For example] The light of pure intelligence shines forth into certain men of holy vision, Which, seated between the two eye brows, illumines the universe, like fire, lightning, or the sun (Degler, 2007:5).

Awareness then as we have previously noted is being "in touch with the spiritual, existential and cosmic realities and sensing and responding to their interconnectedness" (Capra, cited in Spears, 1998:119). According to Degler (2007:5): "Hildegard's profound mystical experience in 1141 was significant not only because it brought with it a greater level of illumination, but also because the voice in the vision commanded her to 'say and write' what she 'saw and heard' in her visions." A leader who fosters awareness is cognizant of the existential reality and endeavours to promote wholeness and harmony [even] where there might be, uncertainty and lack of faith (cited in Cameron, 2012). Butcher writes of the 'Living Light' the 'divine voice' that "sang out to … [Hildegard]":

> I am the living Light. I make the darkness day and have chosen you to see great wonders, though I've humbled you on earth. You're often depressed and timid, and you're very insecure … But the deep mysteries of God have saturated you, too, as has humility. So now you must give others an intelligible account of what you see with your inner eye and what you hear with your inner ear (2013:53).

Gradually Hildegard's self-doubt disappeared and with growing confidence she declared: "that voice made me – a heartbroken, fragile creature – begin to write, though my hand was shaking … I looked to the living Light asking, 'But what should I write down' and that brightness commanded, 'Be simple. Be pure. Write down what you see and hear'" (ibid.)! Greenleaf recommends cultivating awareness: "The cultivation of awareness gives one the basis for detachment, the ability to stand aside and see oneself in perspective in the context of one's own experience" (2002:41). It is then that such a person is able to visualise the future with a readiness to share and serve vision. Joe Batten (cited in Spears, 1998:53; cited in Cameron 2012) quotes Robert Schuller: "The world of tomorrow belongs to the person who has the vision today." Batten refers to 'value-led leaders' as visioneers: "Visioneers stop telling, commanding, and coercing; instead, they ask, listen, and hear."

Hildegard was aware that she was being given a tremendous responsibility and she was concerned that her skills (both written and interpersonal) might let her down. Anzalone (2007:800) emphasises that "the capacity to be open to others requires self-awareness. As we practice self-discovery and reflection, we become more adept at decoding the feelings of others. The path to self-knowledge is not always a smooth one." Newman (1990:12) reminds us that "It took decades of painfully acquired self-knowledge – and the authority of an abbatial position – before she was able to understand the visions as a vehicle for divine revelation." Greenleaf stresses that awareness "is not a giver of solace – it is just the opposite. It is a disturber and an awakener. Able leaders are usually sharply awake and reasonably disturbed. They are not seekers after solace. They have their own inner serenity" (2002:41; cited in Cameron, 2012).

Hildegard's moment of revelation gave her courage but did not allay her fears that she may not be up to the task. She used self-deprecating language when considering the enormity of her responsibilities:

> In the rare text where she portrays herself as a partner in dialogue with God, she is not the enamoured bride longing for divine union as in St. Bernard's *Sermons on the Song of Songs*, but the fragile and woefully inadequate mortal – 'ashes of ashes, and filth of filth' – trembling before the great commission she has received (Newman, 1990:17).

Hoyle quotes Chopra (2002) who "observes that leaders are the symbolic souls of the organizations they lead, and great leaders respond from the higher levels of spirit and grow from the inside out …" Chopra maintains that "by looking inward, any individual has the capacity to rise to greatness … The soul is an archetypal expression of who we are. Everything dynamic about us comes from this deeper level of spirit" (2002:10; cited in Cameron, 2009).

This gift of awareness for discerning the inner spirit led to Hildegard being referred to as a prophet. Benedict (2010a:1) explains:

> The Pope authorised the mystic to write down her visions and to speak in public. From that moment Hildegard's spiritual

prestige continued to grow so that her contemporaries called her the "Teutonic prophetess". This, dear friends, is the seal of an authentic experience of the Holy spirit the source of every charism: the person endowed with supernatural gifts never boasts of them, never flaunts them and above all, shows complete obedience to the ecclesial authority.

According to Newman (1990:17): "Hildegard's prophetic self-awareness pervades all her writings except for her scientific works, and accounts for many of their stylistic features as well as their characteristically objective or outer-directed teaching. Because she saw herself as the voice of another not as a speaker in her own right, she often seems disturbingly unaware of the human element in her writings." Teilhard de Chardin explains that "We are not human beings having a spiritual experience. We are spiritual beings having a human experience" (cited in Stephen Covey, 2004:318; cited in Cameron, 2012). And so it is that a servant leader's awareness "spans all directions all of the time" (Greenleaf, cited in Don Frick and Larry Spears, 1996:76). According to Greenleaf such a leader nurtures the human spirit for their awareness has led to self knowledge and thus 'inspirited' they "take risks and lead more fulfilled lives" (cited in Fraker and Spears, 1996:45). Spiritual leadership is "encouraging others to seek the highest vision, reaching for the highest human endeavours, and serving before being served" (Hoyle, 2007:30).

Newman (1990:16) suggests that according to 'hearsay' much of what Hildegard recorded about her 'inner experience' that is; her awareness of her inner reality which is basically the story of her life has come down to us through the work of Guibert of Gembloux, a Belgian monk. Silvas (1998:xxi) writes that "The first attempts to compile material for a *Vita* (Life) of Hildegard herself took place while both she and Volmar were still alive. To this end, he [Volmar] edited the first systematic collection of her correspondence. It seems likely that it was for Volmar's use in a projected *vita* that Hildegard wrote out, or dictated, her autobiographical notes." Unfortunately Volmar died in 1173 some years before Hildegard who died in 1179. The monk who replaced Volmar was Godfrey who came from Disibodenberg and "who implemented the project and composed a *libellous* or 'little book' of her life, which survives now as the first seven chapters of *VH* [*Vita S. Hildegardis* – The Life of Saint Hildegard]. But Godfrey died in 1176, too soon to finish his projected work" (Silvas, 1998:xxxi).

The search was on then "for another monk to continue recording significant events from the life of Hildegard and so Godfrey's successor, Guibert of Gembloux was appointed to the task" (ibid.) Guibert was:

> [A] learned monk from the monastery of Gembloux in Brabant, who stayed at Hildegard's monastery during the last two or three years of her life, enjoying her trust and friendship ... He canvassed written sources; what he could also from 'Oral Tradition' ... [He engaged in] conversations with Hildegard herself, and with members of the community, as well as interviews [that] he carried out, such as with the monks at Disibodenberg ... After Hildegard died (1179), and while he was still resident at Rupertsberg, Guibert commenced writing the *vita*. But sometime late in 1180, he was suddenly called away, and had to break off his work. He was never able to return to it. But he left the collection of biographical sources behind him, while taking his own unfinished *vita* with him (Silvas, 1998:xxi).

Unfortunately the scholar Theodoric of Echternach, who was 'commissioned' to complete the *Vita – The life of Hildegard* had never met Hildegard and he "was dependent for his knowledge of her solely on the stock of written materials left behind by Guibert"

(Silvas, 1998:xxii). However Silvas maintains that "It was Theodoric who at last brought the project to a conclusion. The end product, *The Life of Holy Hildegard* is without doubt one of the outstanding *vitae* of the century, and something of a literary watershed for its generous inclusion of verbatim autobiographical passages of its subject" (p. xxii). And so the preservation of the documents on the life of Hildegard raises awareness of her life story.

Covey (1990, cited in DeGraaf et al., 2001:10) emphasises the importance of understanding the journey of life and he "encourages personal awareness and 'beginning with the end in mind' in order to understand the big picture of one's life. Covey points out that each part of your life should be examined in the context of the whole, within the context of what really matters most to you." DeGraaf et al. (2001:9) stress that it is important to "realise life while we live it" and they describe awareness as, "Keeping in touch with ourselves and others … [it is] appreciating all that is going on around us and inside of us, to be in touch with other people and ourselves" (ibid.).

You may recall from previous chapters that over the years Hildegard was reticent about divulging the mystical visions she experienced and Degler tells us that "in the Preface to *Scivias* she [Hildegard] explains that this reticence arose out of a combination of humility, self-doubt, and concern for 'evil opinions' – a phrase that might well have alluded to a realistic fear of being accused of witchcraft or possession" (2007:5). And so when commanded by the *Living Light* to record her visions (*Scivias*, 1990:59-60) Hildegard was reluctant and when she persisted in her refusal her health suffered. She became extremely ill. Hildegard referred to this illness as the "scourge of God" and she only regained her health when she responded to advice given to her in her visions. It was then that Hildegard rose from her sick bed aware of what she must do

– she needed to inform the world of the message of the Divine command and so action was required. Brennan (2003:8) quotes Bergson emphasising that "perfect mysticism is action."

Degler contends that Hildegard's knowledge of her self-awareness led her to an awareness of others. She realised that she needed to get the *message* out there:

> The moment she began to do as the voice within the light had commanded, her illness lifted – and one of the most phenomenal creative outpourings in history began. Between her forty-third year and her death at the age of eighty-one, Hildegard produced what can only be called a monumental amount of literary, poetical, musical, medical, and scientific material. In total, she wrote three lengthy books on her visions, two books on medicine, a book depicting the cosmology of the world, two biographies of saints, a morality play, liturgical poetry, and the words and music to a cycle of over seventy songs. She even wrote a mysterious and apparently unfinished dictionary containing the definitions to some 900 words that appear to be from a completely unknown language. Beyond all this, Hildegard expressed herself artistically by overseeing – if not doing some of the work herself – on a great many illustrations that depict elements from her visions (2007:5).

Hildegard's responsibility was to heed the directives of the *Living Light* while at the same time being aware of the spiritual well-being and needs of her sisters in religion. Heider (1985:143) quotes Verse 72 of *the Tao of Leadership*, "Group work must include spiritual awareness if it is to touch the existential anxiety of our times. Without awe, the awful remains unspoken; a diffuse malaise remains … The wise leader models spiritual behaviour and lives in harmony with spiritual values." Hunter (2004:99) also stresses the need for leaders to be aware of the value of all members of the organisation, "Effective leaders understand that everyone is important and adds value to an organization" (cited in Cameron, 2009). Admittedly one person may not accomplish all that Hildegard was able to achieve during her lifetime but just one person can "be the difference that makes a difference" and developing an awareness of self and others will lead each person to be the best they can be in their mission of service to the Church.

Hildegard's profound awareness resulted in her visionary writings which transcend ordinary human knowledge for she had divine inspiration. Her work is prolific and there are few areas that have not been touched by her amazing gifts as is evidenced in the previous paragraphs. And as Abbess she still had time to oversee her sisters in religion. She was what Beare (2006:11) refers to when he discusses leaders with soul: "We want to be led by big-minded, expansive, altruistic people with admirable values, with a robust faith about the nature of things, and with cosmic vision." Hildegard was all these and more. Newman tells us that she was able to "understand the visions as a vehicle for divine revelation … her visions set a seal on the prophetic authority she claimed: without them she would have had neither a message nor an audience. Illness, on the other hand, kept her constantly aware of her human frailty and furnished one of the abiding themes of her spirituality, that of divine power made perfect in weakness" (1990:12).

In his Apostolic Letter proclaiming St Hildegard of Bingen a *Doctor of the Universal Church* Pope Benedict XVI recalls the words of St John Paul II in 1979 on the occasion of the 800th Anniversary of the death of 'this German mystic' when the late Pontiff referred to Hildegard as "A Light for her people and her time" (2012a:1-2). Benedict continues with, "the profound spirituality of her writings had a significant influence both on the faithful and on important figures of her time and brought about an incisive renewal of theology, liturgy, natural sciences and music" (ibid.). Benedict emphasises that Hildegard's works were:

> born from a deep mystical experience and propose a perceptive reflection on the mystery of God ... the Lord endowed her with a series of visions from childhood whose content she dictated to the Benedictine monk Volmar, her secretary and spiritual advisor, and to Richardis von Stade, one of her women religious ... Theological reflection enabled Hildegard to organize and understand, at least in part, the content of her visions ... The range of vision of the mystic of Bingen was not limited to treating individual matters but sought to offer a global synthesis of the Christian faith. Hence in her visions and her subsequent reflections she presents a compendium of the history of salvation from the beginning of the universe until its eschatological consummations (2012a:2-3).

Hildegard's interpretations of her visions then were a result of infused knowledge that had been granted to her as a result of divine revelation. Greenleaf (cited in Fraker and Spears, 1996:4) maintains that "inspired, prophetic institutional leadership begins with one spirit-filled faithful person, who will be strong enough to strike out on a different path, leading the institution down that path" (cited in Cameron, 2009). That person was and is Hildegard of Bingen. Benedict (2012a:1-2) maintains that "her authority reaches far beyond the confines of a single epoch or society; despite the distance of time and culture, her thought has proven to be of lasting relevance ... The corpus of her writings, for their quantity, quality and variety of interests, is unmatched by any other female author of the Middle Ages."

The following Prayer of Awareness was written by Hildegard:

A Prayer of Awareness
Hildegard of Bingen

God is the foundation for everything
This God undertakes, God gives.
Such that nothing that is necessary for life is lacking.
Now humankind needs a body that at all times honors
and praises God.
This body is supported in every way through the earth.
Thus the earth glorifies the power of God.

This prayer was used for Earth Day, 1990. From: Interfaith Declarations and Worship Observance Resources; The North American Conference on Religion and Ecology; 5 Thomas Circle, NW, Washington, DC 20005.

10

Persuasion

As highlighted in Chapter 5 *Persuasion* can be defined as the power to influence. Anzalone writes that a "servant leader leads by persuasion rather than by the power of one's position" (2007:800). And "[t]estimonials by trustworthy, credible people who are similar to the target audience … have a high believability" (Hershey, 1993:3) and "Multiple sources, independent of each other but in support of a particular message, have been shown to be persuasion effective" (ibid.). For witnesses to extraordinary events are commissioned to provide testimonials of their experiences and hence their testimonies can be considered persuasive tools.

In this chapter Hildegard's persuasion techniques are evidenced by testimonials from witnesses to her life and works; through her influence in persuading others to support her endeavours; through her charismatic personality and through her persuasive letter writing. In her book *Jutta & Hildegard: The Biographical Sources* Silvas (1998:xviii) includes information from the document referred to as the *Acta Inquisitionis* which "is the fruit of early efforts made towards Hildegard's canonisation, that is the formal authentication and proclamation of her sanctity." The document lists a "host of miracle reports which would have been forthcoming from witnesses called to give testimony during attempts to have Hildegard canonised" (ibid.). Hershey's definition of the persuasion technique of testimonials is applicable to this discussion where testimonials have been recorded in evidence to promote the cause for the canonisation of Hildegard of Bingen.

The *Acta Inquisitionis* includes a letter from Pope Gregory IX "servant of the servants of God, to his dear sons … to the provost of the greater church … deacon and … scholastic of Saint Peter at Mainz, greetings with our apostolic blessing" (Silvas, 1998:258). This letter was sent in 1228 and contains information regarding a petition by the Benedictine nuns to 'advance' the cause for the canonisation of Hildegard of Bingen who had died in 1179. In his Apostolic Letter proclaiming Hildegard a *Doctor of the Universal Church*, Benedict (2012a:2) refers to her death: "Stricken by illness in the summer of 1179, Hildegard died in the odour of sanctity, surrounded by her sisters at the monastery of Rupertsberg, Bingen, on 17 September 1179."

In his letter of 1228 Pope Gregory IX addresses his ecclesial colleagues and informs them of the petition by the Benedictine nuns:

> … the abbess and sisters of the monastery of St Rupert at Bingen in the diocese of Mainz have petitioned us that, since, by the merits of Hildegard of holy memory, abbess of the said monastery, God had deigned to work many miracles up till now, and still deigns to work them, and she who had only learnt to read the psalter composed many books through the revelation of the Holy Spirit, books which were worthy of being brought to the notice of the Roman Church, we, who heard of her praiseworthy and holy way of life while we were serving in a lesser office together with Leo of worthy memory … ought now to exalt her on earth whom the Lord has honoured in heaven, by canonizing her and inscribing her in the catalogue of the saints … And that, just as the light should not lie hidden in the darkness, and *a city on a mountain should not be hidden* (Mt 5:14) so what God is working through her merits should be brought into the light (cited in Silvas, 1998:258-259).

The nuns had submitted a petition to have Hildegard canonised. Now canonisation is an ecclesial process which prior to 1969 followed strict guidelines and was a lengthy and complicated procedure. However the reforms of Blessed Pope Paul VI in 1969 and Pope St John Paul II in 1983 paved the way for the canonisation process to be simplified (Meagher et al., 1979:616; cited in Cameron, 2009) in contemporary times but as Hildegard was a product of the Church in the twelfth century the process would have involved following the earlier 'stricter' guidelines. Pope Gregory IX agreed to undertake an investigation into the request by the sisters:

> Since she [Hildegard] is said to have so shone with miracles that she is held by all ... to be a saint, we have inclined to the petitions of the sisters above mentioned ... Thus, through our apostolic letter we charge you to undertake on our behalf a diligent enquiry into the truth from witnesses worthy of credence, concerning her history, her way of life, her reputation, her merits, her miracles, and in general all her circumstances, and that what you shall learn, you shall set forth faithfully under your seals, and dispatch to us (Pope Gregory IX, cited in Silvas, 1998:259).

And so a delegation was sent to the monastery of St Rupert. The ecclesiastical representatives met with witnesses "worthy of testimony ... concerning the history, way of life, reputation, merits, signs, and other circumstances of the blessed Hildegard" (Silvas, 1998:259). Apparently some witnesses missed out "not because there were not enough witnesses, but because there was not enough time to give to them all" (ibid.)

You may recall that it is important when interpreting past events to follow a hermeneutic approach (see Chapter 1) to do justice to the data recorded from a time long past, for there needs to be an awareness of the cultural context within which this information is interpreted. The witnesses for the cause of canonisation for Hildegard could very well have embellished some of the stories of her good deeds and works and so their interpretation of the events may be somewhat biased as to her miraculous 'powers'; however it is important to hear some of their stories to gain an idea of the incredible achievements of this remarkable woman.

The following information is found in the *Acta Inquisitionis* and includes the testimony of witnesses called to give evidence:

> THE *MAGISTRA* OF SAINT Rupert in Bingen [at the time] Elysa by name, declared on oath concerning the miracles of Blessed Hildegard, that she saw a demoniac Mechtild … set free at the tomb of Blessed Hildegard … she also saw many epileptics set free there … Those suffering various kinds of recurring fevers were set free at her tomb when they called on her name (cited in Silvas, 1998:259-260).

Many similar cases were recorded by various witnesses who testified under oath including a Prioress 'Agnes', a novice mistress 'Beatrix', a cellarer 'Odilia', a lay-sister 'Hedwig', and a chantress called 'Sophia' – just to name a few; also there was a priest 'Roric' who "saw eighteen demoniacs set free at her tomb when they called on her name … [and] Daniel the priest, on oath, says the same" (cited in Silvas, 1998:260). 'Elysa' when giving her testimony as *Magistra* of Saint Rupert stated that the miracles attributed to Hildegard occurred over a period of "less than thirty years" (ibid.).

Many of the witnesses giving testimony on Hildegard's behalf had been acquainted with her and having known her wanted to influence others as to the high regard in which they held the saint of Bingen. Beatrix (mentioned previously) "said on oath, that when she was twelve years old, she was offered to the same monastery and lived with blessed Hildegard for some time. She saw and heard the holy Hildegard foretell the day of her death before everyone in chapter, and that after her death she saw a blind woman Mechtild from the castle ... receive her sight" (cited in Silvas, 1998:261). Beatrix cites a number of cases where miracles occurred that were performed by Hildegard. Odilia, the cellarer, had lived with Hildegard for some years and also testified under oath to similar stories as had been told by the other witnesses. And Mechtild ... under oath stated that she had been born blind but when her mother who was carrying the child Mechtild approached the boat to meet Hildegard the saint "took up water from the Rhine in her left hand, blessed it with her right and washed the blind eyes with it, so bestowing her with sight" (ibid.)

And "RAPOTO, HENRY AND HUMBERT, citizens of Bingen say on oath, that they saw the blessed Hildegard over many days, and that she cast out demons from all who came to her from their province and from elsewhere, cured epileptics ... and worked many other signs which they themselves saw, and that her holiness should not be doubted" (cited in Silvas, 1998:263). It was stated that the members of the community "confessed on oath that her [Hildegard's] writings really were her own, that is the Book *Scivias, The Book of Life's Merits,* [and] *The Book of Divine Works* which were examined in Paris by masters of theology" (cited in Silvas, 1998:270). Other lesser works were also mentioned and a great number of similar testimonies were recorded but there are too many to be included in this chapter. The process of investigating the cause for canonisation occurred about fifty years after the passing of Hildegard and at that time the community was asked the following:

> why the blessed Hildegard was not working signs of late, [that is fewer miracles were being witnessed] they said that when the Lord showed so many miracles after her death there was so great a gathering of peoples at her tomb, and the monastic life and the divine office were so disrupted by the tumult of the people that it was reported to the lord Archbishop. So he came personally to the place and ordered her to stop the signs (cited in Silvas, 1998:269).

Persuasion is defined by P. Karen Murphy and Patricia Alexander (2004:337) as, "an interactive process through which a given message alters individuals' perspectives by changing the knowledge, beliefs, or interests that underlie those perspectives", on the condition that the individuals are open to the change. And as stated earlier in the chapter testimonials, the charism of a leader and building consensus are all persuasive tools.

Benedict (2010a:1) writes about the gifts Hildegard received from the Holy Spirit "the source of every charism." You may recall that charism is also defined as a persuasive element. Conger et al. (2000:747) maintain that "followers of charismatic leaders could be distinguished by their greater reverence, trust, and satisfaction with their leader and by a heightened sense of collective identity, perceived group task performance, and feelings of empowerment." The followers recognise something 'innate' in the leader which draws from them a positive response to be the best they can be (Hunter, 2004).

As has been previously stated Hildegard would not have known the meaning of the term charism or its German equivalent. O'Donnell (1997:186) suggests that those of us who are members of the contemporary Church have the advantage of "the important teaching of Vatican II on charism" where the gifts of the Holy Spirit are referred to as 'charisms'. For example the following is taken from *The Documents of Vatican II* and cited in Walter Abbott (1967:492): "may the individual, 'according to the gift that each has received, administer it to one another' ... [and] From the reception of these charisms or gifts ... arise for each believer the right and duty to use them in the Church and in the world for the good of mankind and for the upbuilding of the Church" (cited in Cameron, 2009).

You may recall in Chapter 2 when Hildegard decided to relocate her nuns from Disibodenberg to their own convent. It was during the time that she was writing the *Scivias* and God had commanded her in a vision to "move to Rupertsberg, near Bingen on the Rhine, and

[to] set up her own establishment ... [but there was] opposition from the abbot and monks" (Flanagan, 1995:4). Newman as mentioned previously maintains that such obstacles did not deter Hildegard who "Used her family connections to secure the land and a miraculous 'charismatic illness' to persuade the abbot that her departure ... [to Rupertsberg] was the will of God" (cited in Scivias, 1990:13).

Bynum emphasises the importance of this 'charismatic illness' of Hildegard "Recent studies of medieval saints have suggested that certain themes such as the religious significance of illness and the need for charismatic authorization do characterise women's religious experience" (cited in *Scivias*, 1990:3-4). Hildegard wanted the monks to take her seriously so she tried to persuade them that the relocation of the nuns would be in the best interests of all concerned. Baird (2006:29) writes that *"the monks of Mount St Disibod never quite forgave her for her singular act of independence"* and that there are letters that attest to this disapproval.

Bynum maintains that: "Analyses of the structure of women's prose and women's visions ... suggest that particular fears shaped women's intellectual efforts, and that the act of writing itself was often for a woman both service to others and audacious self-integration." Bynum refers to Hildegard's "repeated assertion of female inferiority" (ibid.) and raises the point that:

> Both radical feminists and conservative students of mysticism have queried whether what we have in women's texts from the twelfth to the fifteenth century are women's voices at all ... Some scholars have ... [declared] women's writings either a vague echo of more theoretically powerful works by orthodox males or a species of "false consciousness" that reflect merely patriarchal repression. This position assumes not only that women's courage, serenity, self-sacrifice and loyalty were self-delusion but also that the power to repress is the only effective power in human history (cited in *Scivias*, 1990:4).

Greenleaf (cited in Frick and Spears, 1996:159) speaks of "the legitimate use of power"; the power of persuasion. Sims (1997:ix) maintains that servant power, "functions as a two-way exchange, never as subjugating, dominance; it not only influences others, but is also open to influence." Sims asks the question "What gives power its charge, positive or negative, is the quality of relationships. Those who relate through coercion, or from disregard for the other person, create negative energy. Those who are open to others and who see others in their fullness create positive energy" (1997:113). In his many articles and books Greenleaf (cited in Fraker and Spears, 1996:37) argues that shared power (not solo power) is the essence of servant leadership and that 'gentle' persuasion is preferable to coercion:

> Persuasion stands in sharp contrast to coercion; the use, or threat of use, of covert or overt sanctions or penalties, the exploitation of weaknesses or sentiments, or any application of pressure. Persuasion also stands in sharp contrast to manipulation, guiding people into beliefs or actions that they do not fully understand (ibid.).

Bynum does emphasise however that in her writings "Hildegard directs her audience not to a consideration of woman but to a consideration of humankind … the place of the human person … [in the] divine plan that marches from creation through Christ's incarnation to last judgment and final redemption" (cited in *Scivias*, 1990:5). Benedict reinforces this concept, "The human being exists in both the male and female form. Hildegard recognised that a relationship of reciprocity and a substantial equality between man and woman is rooted in this ontological structure of the human condition" (2012:4).

Hildegard would have been aware of the patriarchal influences that filtered through the writings of her male contemporaries. She may or may not have made a conscious decision to indulge in some form of manipulation to get her message across and to influence her readers because her visionary writings remember are the result of divine revelation, and she had been commanded to "write and speak" to all humankind. Greenleaf defines manipulation as: "not sharply distinct from coercion, but it does rest more on plausible rationalizations than on the threats of sanctions or pressure ... People are manipulated when they are guided into beliefs or actions by plausible rationalizations that they do not fully understand." Charismatic leaders can have a persuasive effect on followers both directly and indirectly – by their influence, expertise and behaviour. Blanchard (2007:109) states, "If people like to be around you, you have personal power ... strong interpersonal skills."

You may recall that in Chapter 7 Hildegard exercised her considerable persuasive skills in trying desperately to convince the ecclesiastical authorities to allow her to keep the young nun Richardis von Stade at her convent even though Richardis had been appointed Abbess at Bassum. Hildegard seemed to leave no stone unturned as it were to explore all the available options including letters to the mother and brother of Richardis; a strongly worded letter to Archbishop Heinrich of Mainz and finally a letter to Pope Eugenius III himself. Though Hildegard's amazing achievements had reached Rome and were acknowledged by the Pope in his reply to Hildegard they were not enough to influence his decision which was to delegate the final decision back to the Archbishop of Mainz – Heinrich.

Conger et al. (2000:748) maintain that: "Charismatic leaders differ from other leaders by their ability to formulate and articulate an inspirational vision and by behaviours and actions that foster an impression that they and their mission are extraordinary." Hildegard was such a charismatic leader and her leadership practices generally had a persuasive influence on her followers. You may recall in Chapter 2 when Hildegard had to inform the monks of her intention to relocate her sisters and "found a new convent on the site of a ruined

Carolingian monastery near Bingen [Rupertsberg]. This plan met with vehement objections from her abbot along with many of the nuns, who were loath to leave their comfortable surroundings for a desolated wilderness" (Newman, 1990:13). However Hildegard finally persuaded a group of the nuns to agree to the relocation. Benedict (2010a:1) maintains that "Her manner of exercising the ministry of authority is an example for every religious community: she inspired holy emulation in the practice of good to such an extent that, as time was to tell, both the mother and her daughters competed in mutual esteem and in serving each other."

Hildegard's influence was such that she communicated with people from all walks of life and they in turn sought her advice. Newman (1990:13) writes that Hildegard having moved to Rupertsberg with her nuns was intent on "securing the welfare of her monastery … with every means at her disposal. She worked to establish monastic discipline by teaching and preaching; supervised construction of the new buildings; obtained gifts and bequests to make her community financially secure." All this activity necessitated an increase in correspondence:

> with the outside world. Hildegard's growing fame brought a constant stream of pilgrims and miracle-seekers, as well as prospective nuns, to the Rupertsberg gates. Most of her correspondents were fellow abbesses, abbots and priests, although there is an impressive sprinkling of secular rulers and prelates, and a less prestigious, though perhaps more revealing, selection of letters to ordinary laymen and women (Newman, 1990:13-14).

Baird (2006) in *The Personal Correspondence of Hildegard of Bingen – Selected Letters* includes communication from and to Popes, Archbishops, clergy, Kings (including an Emperor), Queens (including an Empress), a future saint Bernard of Clairvaux, widows, monks, nuns and laymen and women and others. Butcher (2013:95) cites the

Reverend Frederick Holweck who was "domestic prelate to Pope Pius XI", and who emphasises the tremendous influence of Hildegard for ever though "She denounced the vices of society, of kings, nobles, bishops, and priests in unmeasured terms ... the Emperor, bishops, abbots, and laymen came to ask for her advice." Butcher also adds (ibid.) that "MEDIEVAL LETTERS were not usually the personal communications we think of when we speak today of 'letters' or even 'e-mails'."

When the monk Volmar, secretary, confidant and friend of Hildegard died in 1173 the nuns were left without spiritual guidance. Baird (2006:120) tells us that Hildegard wrote immediately requesting that the Abbot (at Disibodenberg) appoint a new provost to attend to the spiritual affairs of the nuns but "the churlish Abbot Helengerus, with whom Hildegard had had other difficulties, refused to comply" for both the Abbot and Hildegard were of differing opinions for the Sisters believed that because of a previous arrangement with Disibodenberg, they could have their choice of provost. The months turned into a year and still "Hildegard sought desperately for a resolution. As usual, the unshakeable Hildegard ... [was] not to be denied" (ibid.) and she wrote to Pope Alexander III citing her dilemma. In her letter to the Pope, Hildegard, extends her greeting, refers to the parable of the Prodigal son and then goes straight to the crux of the letter:

> Now O gentlest father, my sisters and I bend our knees before your paternal piety, praying that you deign to regard the poverty of this poor little woman. We are in great distress because the abbot of Mount St. Disibod [also referred to in this book as the monastery of Disibodenberg] and his brothers have taken away our privileges and the right of election which we have always had, rights which we have been ever careful to retain. For if they will not grant us reverential and religious men, such as we seek, spiritual religion will be

totally destroyed among us. Therefore, my Lord, for God's sake, help us, so that we may retain the man we have elected to that office (cited in Baird, 2006:121).

Baird (ibid.) tells us that the response of Pope Alexander III was to appoint Hildegard's nephew "Wezelinus, abbot of St Andrew in Cologne … to attend the matter." The outcome was that the abbot "Helengerus assigned the monk Gottfried to Hildegard to serve as provost and secretary" (ibid.). You may recall that information on the monk Godfrey (English for Gottfried) was included in the previous chapter. Suffice to say that the situation was resolved and Godfrey became spiritual adviser and was thus personally acquainted with Hildegard and her nuns. Godfrey began to write Hildegard's *Vita* (life) but died in 1176 before the manuscript was completed.

Remember in Chapter 1 and in the earlier paragraphs in this chapter where there is mention of the need for caution when interpreting some of the data relating to Hildegard especially her miracles. Newman makes the following comments in regard to information contained in Hildegard's correspondence: "It is difficult to evaluate Hildegard's correspondence in its present state, however, since her secretaries edited freely in order to upgrade the status of her associates and enhance her image as an inspired oracle of God – possibly with a view to imminent canonization" (1990:14).

In hindsight such a move by those who were keen to have Hildegard canonised in those early years might seem to have been in vain at the time for it was not until 10 May 2012 some eight hundred and thirty-three years after her death that Hildegard of Bingen was inscribed in the catalogue of saints of the Catholic Church (refer to the 'equivalent canonisation' in Chapter 4).

11

CONCEPTUALISATION

Lawrence Lad and David Luechauer (cited in Spears, 1998:59) stress the importance of a leader being able to keep "in mind the 'big picture', which is about questioning organisational purpose, culture, status quo, and values." Indeed such a leader needs to be proactive and questioning and one who challenges the 'prevailing order'. Spears (2010:28) maintains that conceptualisation "requires discipline and practice." For "The leader who wishes to also be a servant leader must stretch his or her thinking to encompass broader-based conceptual thinking and 'seek to nurture their abilities to dream great dreams'" (ibid.). Essentially, leaders need to focus on the 'big picture' even when confronted with day-to-day realities.

You may recall from Chapter 5 that *Conceptualisation* is about having vision. Anzalone (2007:801) in her discussion on conceptualisation refers to the – "'law of navigation,' 'imparting the vision,' creating a 'living and inspirational vision,' and setting 'the paradigm.'" When there is a mental image of the big picture there is vision. For conceptualisation involves planning and setting a purpose which becomes the mission, this then leads to vision. Anzalone (ibid.) highlights the importance of Covey's emphasis on "leaders expressing voice" in their efforts to share the vision. For Covey (2004, cited in Anzalone, 2007:801) asserts, "voice is a composite of vision, discipline, passion, and conscience. Servant leaders empower others to find their voices and, with blended voices, change happens. This is truly a wonderful metaphor to illustrate conceptualization and the power of influence in the servant-led organization" (ibid.).

Hildegard's conceptualisation skills are evident through her mission, which was to reform the Church through being proactive and questioning. She was not content with the status quo and as you read in this chapter she challenged the 'prevailing order'. Hildegard thought beyond the day-to-day realities to realise her dreams for the future and her vision which was to have a united and reformed Church.

Following Hildegard's formal profession into the Religious life as a teenager (see Chapter 2) Newman (1990:11) writes that "We hear nothing more of her until 1136 when Jutta died and Hildegard [at about the age of thirty-eight] was elected abbess in her stead." Flanagan (1998:4) reveals that "The real turning point in her [Hildegard's] career came a few years later in 1141" when she received a spiritual awakening (see Chapter 9) and the "sudden access of understanding by which she felt able to penetrate to the inner meaning of the texts of her religion."

You may recall that during this visionary experience Hildegard received a divine command to write down her visions but she experienced self-doubt believing that the visions may not have come from God and so she chose not to respond for she "shrank from becoming the butt of common gossip and the rash judgements of others" (Silvas, 1998:141) and as a result her 'fragile' health broke down. According to Silvas (ibid.) "having lain in a wasting illness a long time, in fear and humility she laid bare the cause of her scourge." Initially Hildegard informed the monk Volmar (her secretary) and then Bernard, Abbott of Clairvaux who when he was informed and after some consultation with his colleagues reassured Hildegard of the validity of the revelations and "intervened on her behalf with the pope" (Newman, 1990:13). As a result Hildegard's health improved remarkably. In addition to writing to Bernard, Hildegard had also written to Pope Eugenius III "seeking approval of her writing …

[and Baird informs us that] Here too, for the first time, she makes use of her famous metaphor of herself as a small feather wafted aloft by the breath of God" (Baird, 2006:21):

> To *Pope Eugenius III*
>
> O gentle father, poor little woman though I am, I have written those things to you which God saw fit to teach me in a true vision, by mystic inspiration.
>
> O radiant father, through your representatives you have come to us, just as God foreordained, and you have seen some of the writing of truthful visions, which I received from the Living Light, and you have listened to these visions in the embraces of your heart ...
>
> A part of this writing has now been completed. But still that same Light has not left me, but it blazes in my soul, just as it has from my childhood. Therefore, I send this letter to you now, as God has instructed me... father of pilgrims, hear Him Who is: A mighty king sat in his palace, surrounded by great columns girt with golden bands and beautifully adorned with many pearls and precious stones. It pleased this king to touch a small feather so that it flew miraculously, and a powerful wind sustained it so that it would not fall (Baird, 2006:21-22).

Hildegard received formal recognition of her gifts and papal approval of her writing from Pope Eugenius III. Newman (1990:13) emphasises that "The importance of this papal seal of approval cannot be overestimated. Not only did it increase Hildegard's confidence and security in the face of continuing self-doubt, but it also authenticated her publicly and protected her from the censure she was bound to attract for violating the deuteron-Pauline stricture on female silence and submission." Remember in Chapter 3, St Paul's directive: "women should be silent in the churches. For they are not permitted to speak, but should be subordinate, as the law also says. If there is anything they desire to know, let them ask their husbands at home. For it is shameful for a woman to speak in church" [1 Cor., 14:34].

You may recall that as a result of the divine revelation Hildegard received "infused knowledge of all the books of scripture" (Newman, 1990:12) and so she would have been fully aware of St Paul's precept however she was commanded to write and to speak out for she had a 'mandate from God'. Butcher (2013:11) believes that the decision by Hildegard was only made possible by her receiving papal approval for her writing for "Without it, she would probably have been censured eventually ... for transgressing the prohibitions against public female expression, as written down in the fourteenth chapter of the New Testament epistle 1 Corinthians" which is referenced in the above paragraph. Hildegard's mission was to "speak these things that you see and hear. And write them not by yourself or any other human being, but by the will of Him Who knows, sees and disposes all things in the secrets of His mysteries" (the *Living Light*, cited in the *Scivias*, 1990:59).

Hildegard then began her public ministry and though she took ten years to complete the *Scivias* her life had 'changed forever.' Hildegard was intent on reforming the Church. Remember that this was a period of great trials for the Church with the Cathars the heretical movement gaining momentum. The Cathars "advocated a radical reform of the Church, especially to combat the abuses of the clergy" (Benedict, 2010b:3). Also you may remember the "Emperor Frederic Barbarossa [had] caused a schism in the Church by supporting at least three anti-popes against Alexander III, the legitimate Pope" (ibid.). Benedict (2012a:1) emphasises that Hildegard's public mission was spent "strengthening the Christian faith and reinforcing religious practice, opposing the heretical trends of the Cathars, promoting Church reform through her writings and preaching and contributing to the improvement of the discipline and life of the clerics." Newman (1990:20) elaborates:

> As a reformer Hildegard … did not call for radical change of social or ecclesiastical structures; it was the abuse of authority … that she opposed. Her ideal was a Christendom wherein the secular power would be firmly subordinate to the spiritual, princes and prelates would rule with vigilance and justice, and subjects and layfolk would offer prompt obedience. Yet because her message was largely directed to those in power, and particularly to the ecclesiastical hierarchy, she concerned herself … with the negligence of clerics and the arrogance of rulers … Three issues that particularly concerned her were clerical celibacy, simony and the subservience of prelates to the secular power.

In the *Glossary* to the *Catechism of the Catholic Church* (2000:899), 'simony' is defined as "The buying or selling of spiritual things [favours and/or positions], which have God alone as their owner and master." In his Apostolic Letter proclaiming Hildegard of Bingen a *Doctor of the Universal Church* Benedict (2012a:5) refers to Hildegard's perception of those around her: "[She] saw contradictions in the lives of individual members of the faithful and reported the most deplorable situations. She emphasized in particular that individualism in doctrine and in practice on the part of both lay people and ordained ministers is an expression of pride and constitutes the main obstacle to the Church's evangelizing mission to non-Christians."

Hildegard believed that because of her dialogue with God and the commands to her it was her mission to see to the spiritual and physical welfare of the people. Greenleaf (cited in Fraker and Spears, 1996:45) emphasises, "[O]ur society would be made much stronger and more durable if the now able people in our midst, who see themselves as responsible, would take initiatives and risks to inspirit … institutions and lead them to be more serving."

Hildegard certainly took risks as described in this and the previous chapters. For example, her correspondence was one area where she wrote as a 'leader expressing voice' (refer to the introductory paragraphs in this chapter). You may recall from previous chapters where she is direct in her advice to clergy and laity. It was her intention to reform the Church and she did and said what she could to make this happen confident that she was the spokesperson as it were for the *Living Light*. Butcher (2013:95) claims that "Hildegard prefers to open her letters with the voice of God. She often begins, 'The Living Spring says –' and she likes to close with this reminder … 'This writing doesn't come from any human person, but from the living Light. May all who hear it see and believe in Me.'"

The following excerpts are taken from letters written by Hildegard in her efforts to preach what she had heard and seen in her visions, for the *Living Light* commanded: "Arise therefore, cry out and tell what is shown to you by the strong power of God's help, for He Who rules every creature in might and kindness floods those who fear Him and serve Him in sweet love and humility with the glory of heavenly enlightenment and leads those who persevere in the way of justice to the joys of the Eternal Vision" (cited in *Scivias*, 1990:67).

To the *Abbot of Busendorf* (about 1150):

> Visions often illuminate my soul when I'm completely awake. In one of these, I saw a whirlwind in your monastery. It was really a hurricane, and its lightning and churning black clouds shook the very foundation of your community. I also saw the three colors of your soul. It is black with hatred and anger, and gray with the smoke of perverse hungers. The third color, however, is the dawn-red of goodness that starts in the godly sorrow of repentance … [the] storm is the indolent, spiteful heart of someone who knows what good needs to be done and can make it happen, but who chooses to be lazy and to give in to hatred, instead of doing good works. Son of God, run from these tendencies in yourself… (cited in Butcher, 2013:100).

Hildegard's advice to the Abbot is a warning that if he persists with his inappropriate behaviour he will suffer the consequences however she does point out that there is hope if he responds positively to her advice.

To *King Frederick, later Emperor Barbarossa* (1152 or later): "King! Think before you act. You must learn to do this. I saw you in a spiritual vision, and, before the Living Eye, you looked like either a foolish little boy or a totally insane man. But you still have time to be a ruler. This is your warning" (cited in Butcher, 2013:103). Strong words indeed to a king whom you remember in Chapter 7 felt the 'wrath' of Hildegard but who seems to be tolerant of her behaviour towards him. In the next chapter on *Foresight* is reference to a prophecy that Hildegard successfully foretold and was in the best interests of Frederick which might explain his 'inaction' regarding her disparaging words in his regard.

To the Duke Welf VI of Altdorf (about 1153) "*Also known as Duke Guelf VI*":

> Listen to the Living Eye. God made you a prince in this world, and you're lucky to have this divine legacy, because it means you won't be rejected by God or by the world. So why are you rejecting God's invitation? You do this when you choose immorality. Why do you spend your days bragging, stuffing yourself like a glutton, and getting drunk (ibid.)? A deep darkness also envelops you because you've wronged your marriage … If you don't conquer this fault of yours, you'll be held in contempt by the living light, and you'll never have a son (cited in Butcher, 2013:103).

Hildegard believes that the Duke is living a life of debauchery and that as a leader he should put God and the needs of his family and people before his own self-serving needs. If he persists in his degenerate behaviour the punishment for his inability to comply with the will of God would be that he would have no son to inherit his title.

To *Pope Anastasius IV* (1153 or 1154):

> Bright defender and consummate leader of God's holy city! Listen to the One who lives forever and never wearies. Your wisdom weakens. You're tired, and the people around you are arrogant. Pull up these evil roots, who strangle the flowers and other good plants. You've turned your back on justice, who is God's daughter. She was yours to protect, but you've merely stood by and watched her thrown to the ground by violent men, who trample her clothing and crown … you as pope must never collude with corruption … May you, Father and Shepherd, find the path of justice, because you don't want to be reprimanded by the great Physician for not disciplining your sheep (cited in Butcher, 2013:104-105).

In the above letter from Hildegard to Pope Anastasius IV, Baird (2006:16) notes that Hildegard is "telling the pope flatly that he is too old and tired to conduct his office properly and castigating him for banishing justice from his presence."

To the *Abbess of Bamberg* (After 1157):

> Mother, a person who doesn't plow a field to make it grow crops is negligent. She's shirking her work … Daughter of God, the field is yours. Your goodness embraces those in your care. Don't refuse to be their leader. Don't abandon them just because you want a break from the responsibilities of being an abbess, because weeds that choke good growth thrive in idleness … Discipline your daughters. Make them behave (cited in Butcher, 2013:111)

Hildegard is reprimanding the Abbess for her inability to control her nuns and for taking the easy way out by ignoring what is happening around her. If the Abbess doesn't improve her leadership skills and manage her nuns the situation will continue to deteriorate.

To *Helengerus, Abbot of St. Disibod* (About 1170):

> In a spiritual vision which I received from God, I heard these words: If, amidst his desires, a man wished to find his soul, he must abandon the wicked works of the flesh and affirm that God-given knowledge of the way to conduct his life … Now listen and learn so that in the inwardness of your soul you will be ashamed. Sometimes you are like a bear which growls under its breath; but sometimes like an ass, not prudent in your duties, but, rather, worn down. Indeed, in some matters you are altogether useless … Poor little woman that I am, I see a black fire in you kindled against us, but use your good knowledge to consign it to oblivion, lest the grace and blessing of God depart from you during your time in office (cited in Baird, 2006:32-33).

Helengerus replaced Cuno as Abbot of the monastery at Disibodenberg in 1155 and Hildegard had words with Helengerus when the nuns were keen to elect their own provost (spiritual adviser) following the death of Volmar in 1173. However the above letter is dated some three years earlier so the tension between the two communities would have continued for some time. Hunter (2004:208) maintains that "Community is not a place free from conflict. Indeed, when two or more people are gathered together for a purpose, there will be conflict – at least there should be in a healthy community" (cited in Cameron, 2009).

Flanagan (1998:152) tells us that "it was not as an authority in her own right that Hildegard's opinion and direction was sought, but rather as the agent through which the will of God … [was] to be known." Flanagan also informs us that "The largest surviving body of her correspondence, in a manuscript known as the Riesenkodex, now at Wiesbaden, consists of a series of paired letters in which a letter supposedly written by Hildegard is followed by a reply" (ibid.) However Flanagan says that some licence has been taken with the material and that some letters may have been assimilated with others.

The letters cited from Hildegard in this Chapter are but some of the many she sent to people – some who asked her advice and others who didn't. Her correspondence covered a wide range of topics including – requests for prayers, "for letters of admonition or consolation … general [questions and] … Those concerned with exorcism" (Flanagan, 1998:153). Hildegard took her ministry seriously for she had been appointed by the *Living Light*. Her considerable gifts were recognised. She was praised and her gifts lauded. "[H]er prayers and advice sought by members of the upper clergy in her immediate area and beyond. Moreover such recognition is spread over many years" (Flanagan, 1998:154). Hildegard's magnetic personality spread far and wide:

> The popularity that surrounded Hildegard impelled many people to seek her advice. It is for this reason that we have so many of her letters at our disposal. Many male and female monastic communities turned to her, as well as Bishops and Abbots. And many of her answers still apply for us. For instance, Hildegard wrote these words to a community of women religious: "The spiritual life must be tended with great dedication. At first the effort is burdensome because it demands the renunciation of caprices of the pleasures of the flesh and of other things. But if she lets herself be enthralled by holiness a holy soul will find even contempt for the world sweet and lovable. All that is needed is to take care that the soul does not shrivel" (E. Gronau, 1996:402, cited in Benedict, 2010a:3).

Hildegard was untiring in her quest to proclaim the message of the *Living Light* and so her activities for the Church continued even into her advanced years. In 1158 when about 60 years of age she set out on her preaching tours which were to number three over five years. Newman (1990:14-15) recounts that Hildegard undertook the tours "despite the burden of illness. Travelling along Germany's great rivers, the Rhine and the Main, she preached at numerous monasteries and gave fiery apocalyptic sermons in the cathedral towns of Cologne and Trier." Many of the sermons she preached have come down to us today and "can be found among her correspondence" (ibid.). Butcher goes into a little more detail regarding the state of Hildegard's health and some of the activities in which she engaged on the preaching tours. Each of the three tours was undertaken separately.

For example "Despite persistent ill health (such as exhaustion, fevers, and breathing difficulties), in 1158 she [Hildegard] launched a series of unprecedented preaching tours. She travelled by ship, by horseback, and on foot ... the first tour took her down the Main River, from Mainz east to Bamberg" (2013:15). Butcher lists the towns along this stretch of land visited by Hildegard when she preached to the communities (ibid.). It was during this time that Hildegard commenced her second visionary work *Liber vitae Meritorum* (Book of Life's Merits). This second part of her trilogy of works was completed during the years 1158 to 1163.

In 1160 Hildegard embarked on the second of her three preaching tours. Butcher records that Hildegard:

> travelled west and south along the Rhine River from Trier to Metz, with a trip to the monastic community at Krauftal. At Trier she preached in public, a most unusual venue for a woman of her day, and she delivered her sermon on Pentecost ... Hildegard began it with her usual humble apology for being "a feeble little body lacking health, energy, a bold spirit, and learning," then added that "the mystical Light" had told her to chide the Trier prelates for shirking their duties and not blowing "the trumpet of justice," a negligence on their part that, she said, darkened earth's bright dawns and turned virtue's compassion into the coldest bitterness" (2013:15).

Benedict (2010a:3) refers to the preaching tours of Hildegard stating that "Hildegard set out ... despite her advanced age and the uncomfortable conditions of travel ... to speak to the people of God. They all listened willingly, even when she spoke severely: they considered her a messenger sent by God. She called ... the clergy to a life of conformity with their vocation."

It was about 1161 that Hildegard embarked on her third preaching tour. It is thought that she travelled north along the Rhine stopping at towns along the way until she reached Cologne. "At Cologne, as at Trier, she preached thundering apocalyptic sermons to both clergy and lay people" (Butcher, 2013:15-16). Hildegard's audiences gathered to hear her in the "monasteries, churches, and public venues such as village marketplaces" (ibid.). As noted in Chapter 7 the clerics of Cologne, who were the recipients of the fiery sermon requested Hildegard put the sermon into written form so that they would remember what the 'oracle of God' had requested of them to transform their lives.

It was during these very busy years of increased activity on behalf of the Church (1163-1173) that Hildegard commenced the third book in what is referred to as the trilogy of her visionary works – the *Liber Divinorum Operum* (Book of Divine Works). Hildegard's visionary thinking led to her visionary works. She had vision she had spirit. Greenleaf (cited in Fraker and Spears, 1996:125) emphasises that spirit needs to be recognised "as an essential ingredient of leadership." Greenleaf continues:

> Spirit in a leader is the quality that leads him or her into risk and venture. Spirit directs the leader when the going gets tough, uncertain, or hazardous and gives strength and assurance to the less hardy. Spirit sustains the leader in long, depressing periods when things are not going well. Spirit arms the leader for the stress of crisis and the unexpected. Spirit is an aspect of inner strength (ibid.).

The preaching tours undertaken by Hildegard would have been a challenge for a younger more able person but she was determined to let the light that was within her shine so that her ministry of leadership would be illumined by the *Living Light*. Hence Hildegard's conceptual thinking enabled her to share her visionary works and serve others while preaching her mission for a reformed Church.

12

FORESIGHT

Foresight and conceptualisation are closely related. DeGraaf et al. (2001:15) posit that "Conceptual skills allow us [to] see the big picture, the *where we want to go*. Foresight allows us to map out how we are going to get there by anticipating the various consequences of our actions and then picking the actions that will serve us best." Anzalone (2007:802) emphasises that foresight is a characteristic needed if an individual "wishes to lead an organization forward. Moving toward a goal requires leaders who are acutely aware of the present, able to learn from history, and able to divine possible consequences of proposed future actions … Leadership requires imagination."

Greenleaf (2002:35) writes about requirements for leadership and maintains that those who aspire to leadership require two intellectual abilities *"The leader needs to have a sense for the unknowable and be able to foresee the unforeseeable.* Leaders know some things and foresee some things that those they are presuming to lead do not know or foresee as clearly. This is partly what gives leaders their 'lead,' what puts them out ahead and qualifies them to show the way." In other words a leader needs to be intuitive (cited in Cameron, 2009).

Hildegard demonstrated Foresight through her visionary leadership and her prophetic gifts. Pope Benedict XVI (2010a:1-2) refers to Hildegard as a "'prophetess' who also speaks with great timeliness to us today, with her courageous ability to discern the signs of the times, her love for creation, her medicine, her poetry, her music … her love for Christ and for his Church which was suffering in that period too, wounded also in that time by the sins of both priests and lay people."

You may recall that people corresponded with Hildegard for many and varied reasons. Flanagan (1998:154-155) makes reference to Hildegard's 'monastic correspondents' and suggests that there are some who "make explicit mention of Hildegard's prophetic gifts." Flanagan quotes from a letter to Hildegard by "Adam of Ebrach … expressing his concern about how to care for his monks, [and] refers in closing to 'the gift of the Holy Spirit, which works many marvels in you by the spirit of prophecy'" (ibid.). Again quoting from a letter to Hildegard from Ludwig of St Eucharius … "you surpass in keenness of mind not only philosophers and dialecticians, but even the prophets of old." Flanagan (1998:155) suggests that Hildegard's prophetic gift enabled her to foresee the future and that "Although there are many difficulties in dating individual letters, her [Hildegard's] correspondence covers the years from around the Council of Trier [in 1148] to the end of her life" (p. 214).

In 2010 some eight hundred and thirty-one years after the death of Hildegard and prior to her 'equivalent canonisation' and proclamation as a *Doctor of the Universal Church* in 2012 Pope Benedict XVI quoted from a letter that Hildegard sent to Abbot Werner von Kirchheim and His Priestly Community in response to his request. In his earlier correspondence Abbot Werner of Kirchheim "notes that her [Hildegard's] reputation depends not only on the performance of good works but also on her knowledge of the future. His specific request is for a copy of a sermon Hildegard preached 'to us and many more in Kirchheim about the failings of priests'" (Flanagan, 1998:155).

Hildegard's response to Abbot Werner von Kirchheim is included in Pope Benedict's Address to the Roman Curia in December 2010. The celebration of the Year for Priests had concluded earlier in June 2010, and Benedict (2010c:2) spoke with great appreciation for the wonderful work being accomplished by priests emphasising "there was a renewed awareness of what a great gift the lord has entrusted to us in the priesthood of the Catholic Church." The Pope then spoke about how difficult a year it had been for the Church "We were all the more dismayed, then, when in this year of all years and to a degree we could not have imagined, we came to know of abuse of minors committed by priests who twist the sacrament into its antithesis, and under the mantle of the sacred profoundly wound human persons in their childhood, damaging them for a whole lifetime" (ibid.). It was then that Pope Benedict referred to Hildegard's letter to Abbot Werner von Kirchheim saying that what is expressed by Hildegard (over eight centuries ago) describes "in a shocking way what we have lived through this past year" (2010c:2):

> In the year of our Lord's incarnation 1170, I had been lying on my sick-bed for a long time, when fully conscious in body and in mind, I had a vision of a woman of such beauty that the human mind is unable to comprehend. She stretched in height from earth to heaven. Her face shone with exceeding brightness and her gaze was fixed on heaven. She was dressed in a dazzling robe of white silk and draped in a cloak, adorned with stones of great price. On her feet she wore shoes of onyx. But her face was stained with dust, her robe was ripped down the right side, her cloak had lost its sheen of beauty and her shoes had been blackened. And she herself, in a voice loud with sorrow, was calling to the heights of heaven, saying, "Hear, Heaven, how my face is sullied: mourn, earth, that my robe is torn; tremble, abyss, because my shoes are blackened!"
>
> And she continued: "I lay hidden in the heart of the Father until the Son of Man, who was conceived and born in virginity, poured out his blood. With that same blood as his dowry, he made me his betrothed.
>
> For my Bridegroom's wounds remain fresh and open as long

as the wounds of men's sins continue to gape. And Christ's wounds remain open because of the sins of priests. They tear my robe, since they are violators of the Law, the Gospel and their own priesthood; they darken my cloak by neglecting in every way, the precepts which they are meant to uphold; my shoes too are blackened, since priests do not keep to the straight paths of justice, which are hard and rugged, or set good examples to those beneath them. Nevertheless, in some of them I find the splendour of truth."

And I heard a voice from heaven which said: "This image represents the Church. For this reason, O you who see all this and who listen to the word of lament, proclaim it to the priests who are destined to offer guidance and instruction to God's people and to whom, as to the apostles, it was said: go into all the world and preach the Gospel to the whole creation" (Mk 16:15; *Letter from Hildegard to Werner von Kirchheim and his Priestly Community: PL* 197, 269ff.).

Benedict (2010b:3) emphasises that during her public life the clergy listened willingly to the words of Hildegard "even when she spoke severely ... [for] they considered her a messenger from God." Her message being that they should live "a life in conformity with their vocation" (ibid.). Flanagan reminds us that it is in Hildegard's "letters from clergy, monks, and nuns ... [that her] prophetic powers are ... more clearly implied. Thus almost one quarter of the letters ask either about the present state of the writer's soul (often in conjunction with the state of his or her monastery) or its ultimate fate" (1998:157).

Butcher recounts words the *Living light* speaks to Hildegard in the third part of her visionary trilogy *The Book of Divine Works*. The content refers to *The Signs of the End Times*:

The Son said to his Father, "In the beginning, Creation was green, It flowered." That was a virile time, but now we live in a time of womanly infirmity, because everyone does only as they please. No one does what is right, and the Church is abandoned, like a widow who has lost the companionship of her husband, who once protected her and helped her.

Instead, evil clergy prostitute themselves for money. They're a stumbling block for My flock. They keep My little ones in the valleys and don't help them climb up the mountains. Their main goal is to accumulate money. They want diamond rings and other riches. They're greedy wolves who follow sheep tracks, killing those they can and scattering those they can't catch (2013:157).

Dire words of warning not just for the Church and clergy but for all who put love of mammon (riches/wealth) before their love of God and neighbour. Regarding the clergy and money you may remember the reference to simony in the previous chapter. Benedict acknowledges Hildegard's "love for Christ and for his Church which [as we can see] was suffering in that period too, wounded also in that time by the sins of both priests and lay people" (2010a:2).

Hildegard's vision was for a reformed Church. Flanagan again commenting on Hildegard's correspondents maintains that "Hildegard was consulted by members of the monastic orders and secular clergy on a wide range of subjects: from theological questions and matters of personal salvation, to problems of monastic discipline and church organization" (1998:58). And as mentioned in previous chapters her letters were not just to the clergy or to those in religious life but to people in secular life as well – royalty and commoners alike. Benedict (2012a:5) stresses that "The teaching of the holy Benedictine nun stands as a beacon … for [all men and women on their journey through life]. Her message appears extraordinarily timely in today's world."

The *General Directory For Catechesis* (1998:para.46) includes the statement that "The Church 'exists in order to evangelize' that is 'the carrying forth of the Good News to every sector of the human race so that by its strength it may enter into the hearts of men and renew the human race.'" This is also a directive received by Hildegard over eight hundred years ago. Bynum (1990:6) refers to the evangelising mission of Hildegard when she quotes from Hildegard's 'parable of the apostles' in Part III of Vision Number 7 in the *Scivias* which Bynum suggests provides a description of Hildegard's prophetic role:

> And so ... the Holy Spirit came openly in tongues of fire ... And, because the apostles had been taught by the Son, the Holy Spirit bathed them in Its fire, so that with their souls and bodies they spoke in many tongues; and, because their souls ruled their bodies, they cried out so that the whole world was shaken by their voices.
>
> And the Holy Spirit took their human fear from them, so that no dread was in them, and they would never fear human savagery when they spoke the word of God; all such timidity was taken from them, so ardently and so quickly that they became firm and not soft ... And then they remembered with perfect understanding all the things they had heard and received from Christ...
>
> And so, going forth, they made their way among the faithless peoples who did not have roots ... And to these they announced the words of salvation and of true faith in Christ.

Hildegard's foreknowledge of events in the lives of the men and women with whom she corresponded is explained by Newman (1990:12) as resulting from the 'prophetic call' she received during the vision in 1141 which is referred to in Chapter 9 as her 'Spiritual Awakening'. Newman maintains that it was this 'prophetic call' that "eventually led her to compose the *Scivias* and embark on her public mission ... [she had] a propensity for visions from earliest childhood. She could see things that were invisible to those around her; she foretold the future" (Newman, 1990:11).

Flanagan relates a 'tale' from Hildegard's childhood where she demonstrated amazing insight. The occasion concerned "a prescient conversation she had about an unborn calf with her nurse ... The nurse, amazed at her description of the calf as 'white and marked with different coloured spots on its forehead, feet and back', told Hildegard's mother" (1998:24). And when the calf was born the colour and markings were as Hildegard had foretold. Greenleaf (2002:38) believes that, "Prescience, or foresight, is a better than average guess about what is going to happen ... in the future. It begins with a state of mind about now ... the prescient person has a sort of 'moving average' mentality ... in which past, present, and future are one, bracketed together and moving along ... [in time]. The process is continuous."

Newman writes about the exceptional gifts of Hildegard – she was: "The bearer of a unique and elusive visionary charism, she was also a prophet in the Old Testament tradition – the first in a long line of prophetically and politically active women – yet at the same time a representative of the German Benedictine aristocracy in its heyday" (1990:9). Hildegard was persistent and "Her sheer force of will, combined with a dazzling array of spiritual and intellectual gifts, a courage hardened by decades of struggle, and a prophetic persona ... made her a formidable opponent" (p. 15).

It was this 'prophetic persona' that resulted in Hildegard being summoned to the palace of the Emperor Frederick Barbarossa at Ingelheim in about 1155: "to give a prophetic oracle, the contents which neither party ever disclosed in writing" (Newman, 1990:15). The following is taken from a letter sent by Frederick to Hildegard and refers to their meeting at Ingelheim:

> We write to notify you, holy lady, that your predictions came true, exactly as you said they would when we invited you to our court at Ingelheim. With all our might, we will work to

honor our kingdom. Dear lady, we ask that you continue to pray for us and the sisters, too, that we will know God's grace (Butcher, 2013:13).

As Newman states there is no mention of the actual events that have been foretold only that Frederick seems happy with the outcome of Hildegard's prediction.

You may recall towards the end of the previous chapter when Hildegard undertook her preaching tours when she was at Trier and Cologne "she preached thundering apocalyptic sermons to both clergy and lay people" (Butcher, 2013:16). Newman sums up this aspect of Hildegard's personality and how it became interpreted in due course:

> By later medieval generations she was remembered primarily as an apocalyptic prophet. Her fiery but enigmatic writings about the Antichrist and the last stage of world history were collected by a Cistercian monk in 1220 and continued to circulate until the Reformation, when she was perversely hailed as a proto-Protestant because she had prophesied the confiscation of ecclesiastical wealth by princes and the dissolution of the monasteries.

As mentioned by Newman the threat to the Church in "later medieval generations" was the spread of Protestantism (Kieran Kavanaugh and Otilio Rodriguez, 1980:20). For it was in the sixteenth century that protestors reacted to calls for reform and renewal in the Church by engaging in and establishing a religious movement which became known as the Reformation. This movement saw the establishment of Protestant Churches. The Catholic response to the Reformation was a Counter Reformation (Gillian Ahlgren, 1996:1, cited in Cameron, 2009).

To be effective a leader must be intuitive and know instinctively when a response is needed to a particular situation. The leader should be able to then discern if action or inaction is required. Newman

(1990:11) emphasises that Hildegard "experienced visions for forty years before receiving her prophetic call and learning to interpret them as a gift from God." Newman continues:

> Unlike modern historians Hildegard did not perceive the mid-twelfth century as a time of spiritual fervor and renewal, but as an 'effeminate age' in which the Scriptures were neglected, the clergy 'lukewarm and sluggish' and the Christian people ill-informed. Her mission, then, was to do with her prophetic charism what professional clerics had failed to do with their priestly charism: teach, preach, interpret the Scriptures and proclaim the justice of God (p. 12).

Hildegard was ready to assume the mantle of leadership for she was illumined with the spirit of the *Living Light*. Greenleaf (Fraker and Spears, 1996:5) maintains, "The effective religious leader, like other leaders, is apt to be highly intuitive in making judgments about what to do and what not to do. Such a leader also draws heavily on inspiration [experience and foresight] to sustain spirit."

Hildegard was informed by the spirit. For example, Silvas (1998:163) writes that "She saw in spirit the past life and conduct of people, and in the case of some, she could even foresee the way their present life would end, and according to the character of their conduct and merits, their soul's glory or punishment." You may recall in the introductory paragraphs of this chapter where Newman refers to Hildegard receiving a 'prophetic call' and it was during this 'spiritual awakening' that Hildegard was given an "infused knowledge of all the books of Scripture" (1990:12). Baird cites letters from a provost and from a monk Godfrey that reveal that it is taken for granted that Hildegard does not have to hear all the details of a person's 'fall from grace' as it were, for the 'sinner' believes that the spirit has kept her informed. In the first letter the provost is quite remorseful and can:

> scarcely find the words to express my misery, my confusion

and shame, my tears of distress. And no wonder! For my body and spirit were sinfully polluted ... So, saintly lady, I cast myself at your feet, since 'I am dust and ashes' ... please inform me whether I have any hope for salvation: am I predestined for life or foreknown for death ... May the Holy Spirit, who dwells in you, grant you to respond to all these things (cited in 2006:56-57).

The provost is asking Hildegard for her assistance as he has committed 'horrible' sins. A second letter is from the monk Godfrey who Baird (2006:57) describes as *"a poor, disconsolate soul who seeks comfort in a word from Hildegard."* Baird states that *"The letter is eloquent testimony of Hildegard's growing fame as prophet and seer, which is spreading widely by word of mouth. 'I have heard of your reputation, which is spreading abroad ... I would walk barefoot just to hear the sound of your voice'"* (ibid.). Baird maintains that Godfrey has only heard of the marvels that have been performed by Hildegard and that he hasn't read any of her works. But according to Baird Godfrey "is confident that she knows all the secrets of his heart, since she sees 'all things past, present, and future'" (ibid.).

Spears (1998:5) stresses the intuitive qualities of foresight and maintains that foresight: "enables the servant-leader to understand the lessons from the past, the realities of the present and the likely consequence of a decision for the future." The evidence from the literature cited in this chapter suggests that Hildegard possessed these qualities.

There are many such examples of prophecies attributed to Hildegard and in 1220c an anthology of Hildegard's prophesies was compiled. It is referred to as the *Pentachronon* – 'The Book of Five Times' or 'Mirror of Future Times' (Magda Hayton, 2015: Abstract).

13

STEWARDSHIP

Stewardship is about empowerment (Anzalone, 2007:803) and that "To be empowered, a follower must first be willing to accept the responsibility of accountability." Being accountable and recognising the need for change to sustain viability in the future is what determines responsible stewardship for this value-driven approach doesn't just happen. In the words of Spears (1998:xiv), "You must work with people to give them a new concept of their stewardship and redefine leadership as service and stewardship."

"The origin of the term *steward* can be traced back to ancient Greece":

> The Greek term for steward is *oiko-nomus* – *oiko* meaning *house* and *nomus* meaning *order*. Thus, the steward can be thought of as the manager of the household. Historically, the word *stewardship* means to *hold something in trust for another* … In today's society, stewardship is often associated with environmental or financial responsibility … stewardship demands constantly addressing two questions: whom do we serve, and for what purpose (DeGraaf et al., 2001:18/19).

Spears (2010:29) emphasises that "Servant leadership, like stewardship, assumes first and foremost a commitment to serving the needs of others." McCuddy and Pirie (2007:961-963; cited in Cameron, 2012) state that Stewardship "has both secular and spiritual implications", and they interpret stewardship as a form of service to others "[It] revolves around service to mankind" (ibid.). This service involves looking after all resources human and non-human, "that God has entrusted to our care" and maintaining these resources to benefit all generations. These sentiments are endorsed by Pope Francis who on the occasion of formally beginning his papacy in March 2013 in his homily called on leaders in all fields "to protect people and the environment."

To have a sense of stewardship is to have an awareness of the sense of connectedness that exists between the inner self and the world. Ann McGee-Cooper (Spears, 1998:77; cited in Cameron, 2012:34) suggests "a new paradigm is emerging through which accountability [responsibility] ... is based on a shared vision." McGee-Cooper refers to this 'shared vision' as a 'covenant.' Such an agreement is based on "Creating a shared vision and agreeing on core values and mission." A servant leader is prepared to share and serve vision.

Hildegard was steward of the "human and institutional resources entrusted to her care" (Stubbs, cited in Spears, 1998:316) and she demonstrated this stewardship through her quest to reform the Church and the clergy, through the legacy of her writings and through her foundations of which there were two – the Rupertsberg convent (founded in 1150) and a convent at Eibingen (founded in 1165).

The Church in the twelfth century was experiencing less than favourable times. For there were "schisms and religious foment, when someone preaching any outlandish doctrine could instantly attract a large following. Hildegard was critical of schismatics, indeed [throughout] her whole life she preached against them, especially the Cathars" (Fordham University Online, p. 2). Silvas gives some idea of reasons behind the movements of monastic and Church reform as she describes events occurring during the papacy of Pope Gregory VII (1073-1085) who led the monastic/church reform during the latter part of the eleventh century. The papacy of Gregory VII occurred some years before the birth of Hildegard in 1098. Silvas maintains that the monastic/church reform led by Gregory:

[A]imed at combating the lay investiture of bishops (i.e. Emperors and kings choosing bishops and investing them with the insignia of office), the practice of simony (the spiritual goods of the church subject to bribery and commercial dealing), the restoration of the ancient canons requiring the celibacy of diocesan priests and of course the moral reform of diocesan clergy (2012:3).

Silvas believes that "Saint Hildegard of Bingen fits precisely into the pro-monastic reform, pro-Church reform, pro-papal movement of her time, which was opposed to the Salian dynasty that currently supplied the current line of German Emperors" (2012:4). Silvas gives her reasons "Hildegard's spiritual mother, Blessed Jutta von Sponheim, was the sister of Count Meinhard, who in 1125, took part in the defeat of the Salian dynasty, by helping elect a new king of Germany, Lothair II, who became Holy Roman Emperor in 1133. In fact he [Lothair] was Jutta and Meinhard's second cousin" (ibid.). Silvas also contends that "It was Hildegard's century that saw the eventual passing of that impulse of monastic reform from the central concerns of the papacy" (1998:5) and that this did not result in a good outcome for the Church: "Part of the tragedy of the Church in the late Middle Ages was that the Papacy became dis-yolked from the monastic cause, and the Church lost her impetus for reform at the highest quarters" (ibid.).

Hildegard was sympathetic to the Church during its time of need. She was also keen to have her visions sanctioned by the Church and this was eventually achieved with the assistance of her secretary the monk Volmar, Abbot Bernard of Clairvaux and finally Pope Eugenius III. Obtaining ecclesiastical approval gave Hildegard the formal recognition and impetus to proceed with her writing. Hildegard assumed custodianship of her works and they have since become her legacy to the Church. Newman discusses the *Scivias* (1141-1151), the first major work of Hildegard and states that "during her lifetime it remained the best known of all her works" (1990:22). Newman notes: "The *Scivias* resulted directly from Hildegard's prophetic call and was addressed to a largely clerical and monastic audience" (ibid.).

At one of two general audiences on Hildegard in September 2010 Pope Benedict XVI (2010b:2) discusses the *Scivias* stating that in ... [Hildegard's] visions she sums up:

> the events of the history of salvation from the creation of the world to the end of time ... Hildegard develops at the very heart of her work the theme of the mysterious marriage between God and humanity that is brought about in the Incarnation. On the tree of the Cross take place the nuptials of the Son of God with the Church, his Bride, filled with grace and the ability to give new children to God, in the love of the Holy Spirit (cf.Visio tertia:PL 197, 453c).

Butcher (2013:51) also refers to the *Scivias* as Hildegard's most "well-known work" citing as a reason that the "fame [may have] resulted in part from the apocalyptic visions of its unforgettable conclusion." Butcher then describes this conclusion: "First the antichrist rapes the allegorized female *Ecclesia* (the Church). Later, the antichrist is sitting on top of a mountain of excrement, which signifies sin's disgusting nature, when a single, divinely sent lightning-bolt knocks this self-exulting imposter down dead" (ibid.). Harsh words for a harsh reality – the Church of the times was 'suffering' but what of the contemporary Church and the Church of the future? What is Hildegard predicting for the Church in her 'prophetic voice'? Hildegard herself cautioned against changing her words: "whoever rashly conceals these words written by the finger of God, madly abridging them, or for any human reason taking them to a strange place and scoffing at them, let him/[her] be reprobate; and the finger of God shall crush him/[her]" (cited in the *Scivias*, 1990:536).

Hildegard does however offer hope to humanity for after the darkness comes light and goodness will prevail:

> *And suddenly from the East a great brilliance shone forth; and there, in a cloud, I saw the son of man, with the same appearance He had had in the world and with His wounds still open, coming with the angelic choirs … He blessed the just in a gentle voice and pointed them to the heavenly kingdom, and with a terrible voice condemned the unjust to the pains of Hell* (cited in the *Scivias*, 1990:515).

Hildegard's works – her eminent doctrine – have been held in trust over many generations. This stewardship of her resources by members of the Benedictine Order has enabled Hildegard's message to be read and heard across the centuries. For as a Doctor of the Universal Church her teaching is relevant not just for her own times but for all time.

You may recall that the works of Hildegard were discussed in Chapter 4. It is opportune now to gain further insight into her major works particularly the trilogy of her visionary writings for these are her legacy to all generations. The *Scivias* as you are aware is the first in Hildegard's trilogy of Visionary works and Pope Benedict XVI (2010b:2) in his second General Audience on Hildegard on 8 September 2010 highlights her other two works – the *Liber Vitae Meritorum* (Book of the merits of life) and the *Liber Divinorum Operum* (Book of the divine works), also called *De Operatione Dei*:

> In the [Book of the merits of life] she describes a unique and powerful vision of God who gives life to the cosmos with his power and his light. Hildegard stresses the deep relationship that exists between man and God and reminds us that the whole creation, of which man is the summit, receives life from the Trinity. The work is centred on the relationship between virtue and vice, which is why human beings must face the daily challenge of vice that distances them on their way towards God and of virtue that benefits them. The invitation is to distance themselves from evil in order to glorify God and, after a virtuous existence, enter the life that consists "wholly of joy."

Newman (1990:15) notes that when Hildegard completed the above work she was "sixty-five and in constant ill health." And though she was producing "remarkable literary work" her strong will was not conducive to promoting friendships. However leadership is not always about being someone's best friend. There are times when tough decisions have to be made. Being accountable and recognising the need for change to sustain viability in the future is what determines responsible stewardship for this value-driven approach doesn't just happen (Cameron, 2012). In the words of Spears (1998:xiv), "You must work with people to give them a new concept of their stewardship and redefine leadership as service and stewardship." Hildegard took five years to write 'The Book of the Merits of Life' and was about sixty years old when she started. Butcher (2013:136) recounts this moment in Hildegard's life:

> When I was sixty, I saw another powerful vision. It was wondrous and I worked five years to write it down ... I heard a voice speaking to me from heaven. It said: "visions have been your teacher since your earliest days. Some of your visions were like milk, other like semi-liquid baby food, and still others like solid food. Articulate now what you hear Me say. Don't rely on yourself. Write down what you see and hear. So I did.

Benedict (2010b:2) in his *Reflection* on Hildegard also discusses the third book in the trilogy of Hildegard's visionary works – her 'Book of divine works'. Benedict states that this book is considered by many to be Hildegard's 'masterpiece' and her emphasis in the book is on:

> creation in its relationship with God and the centrality of the human being, expressing a strong Christo-centrism with a biblical-Patristic flavour. The Saint, who presents five visions inspired by the Prologue of the Gospel according to St John, cites the words of the Son to the Father: "The whole task that you wanted and entrusted to me I have carried out

successfully, and so here I am in you and you in me and we are one" (Pars III, Visio X:PL 197, 1025a).

Newman (1990:21) writes of Hildegard's interest in history and emphasises that "in both the *Scivias* and the *Liber Divinorum Operum* she surveyed the course of salvation history from beginning to end, from the creation to the final judgment … her scenario for the last times represents neither a gradual improvement nor a progressive deterioration in the state of the world." As with the *Scivias* the 'Book of Divine Works' took Hildegard ten years to complete. And when it was completed in 1173 Hildegard was seventy-five years old. According to Butcher (2013:149) "Some call … [this] her best, most mature visionary creation. It presents ten visions in three parts: God's love for the world He single-handedly created, humanity's unique responsibilities and future judgment, and salvation history." Butcher records the words spoken to Hildegard in a vision prior to writing her third visionary work:

> Depressed child of God and daughter of much hard work, even though you've been thoroughly seared – so to speak – by endless terrible pains in your body, the deep mysteries of God have completely infused you. Give others an accurate account of what you see with your inner eye and what you hear with your soul's inner ear. Your testimony will benefit others. As a result, men and women will learn how to get to know their creator, and they'll no longer refuse to adore God with excellence and respect (2013:151).

Though ill Hildegard began to write "That voice made me – heartbroken and fragile creature that I am – begin to write with a trembling hand, even though I was traumatized by more illnesses than I could count. As I started this task, I looked to the true and living Light and asked, 'What should I write down'" (cited in Butcher, 2013:152)? The 'voice' that Hildegard heard with her 'inner ear' and the vision she saw with 'the inner eye of her spirit' is encouraging men and women to know and show respect to the creator. Respect builds trust. Greenleaf (cited in Frick and Spears, 1996:160) emphasises the importance of mutual trust and respect in reference to leadership as a service to others: "Never take anything from anybody, from any situation, without leaving something of greater value than you take away. Never enter a situation without respect for the integrity of [the] personality of every individual involved" (cited in Cameron, 2009).

Apart from her trilogy of visionary works and other minor pieces of writing (as mentioned in Chapter 4) you will recall that Hildegard also produced medical works – the *Causae et Curae* and the *Physica*. Throop (1998) writes that "The Modern reader interested in natural healing will recognize the enormous truth in the theories of this twelfth-century physician." Attending a recent (May 2015) performance on the life and music of Hildegard this writer met enthusiasts who spoke of the wonders of using natural healing remedies recommended by Hildegard. What a wonderful testament to her legacy that her talents and skills have been preserved and safeguarded by the members of her Order and that this 'stewardship' has enabled contemporary admirers of Hildegard's work to be discussing her natural remedies that are still being applied and hearing her music which is still being played more than eight hundred years after her death!

Regarding her natural healing remedies and her writing on the healing systems involving "plants, Elements, Trees, Stones, Fish, Birds, Animals, Reptiles and Metals" environmentalists in the twenty-first century may assume that they have an advocate in Hildegard but according to Flanagan (1995) and as mentioned in Chapter 1 "environmentalism as such would not have been a consideration in Hildegard's era." Even stewardship as it is defined in this chapter would not have been a familiar term for the saint of Bingen though its reference to caring for human and institutional resources would have been acknowledged by Hildegard. Flanagan (1998:77) maintains that "She [Hildegard] elucidated the nature of man, the elements and different creatures and told how humankind is to be served by them (*Vita*, Bk 2)." It is important to remember also that the "*Physica* and *Causa et curae* are distinguished from Hildegard's other works by not being presented in visionary form or containing any reference to a divine source for their contents. Nowhere does she attribute her knowledge of these matters to any kind of revelation" (Flanagan, 1998:78).

In Chapter 1 in the discussion on the leadership practices of Hildegard there is reference to various leadership paradigms apart from servant leadership and mention is made of a twenty-first century leadership paradigm that is becoming popular within leadership circles today and this is the ecology of leadership (Boyd, 2012). Such leadership is about awareness and responding to the call to leadership. It is about motivating people to change so that they are constantly aware of the need to operate in a sustainable manner in order to minimise any and all impact on the environment. When people are suitably motivated they work together as a team, "being effective in today's organizations is a team game, and without collaboration and teamwork skills, you are unlikely to be successful" (Blanchard, 2007; cited in Cameron, 2009).

Spears (1998) emphasises that "You must work with people to give them a new concept of their stewardship and redefine leadership as service and stewardship." Whether a leader refers to an approach to leadership as the ecology of Leadership or servant leadership or one of the many other approaches to leadership (and there are many) Senge (1996) maintains that leaders must create "an environment in which people are open to new ideas, responsive to change, and eager to develop new skills and capabilities." Being accountable and recognising the need for change to sustain viability in the future is what determines responsible stewardship and this value-driven approach doesn't just happen.

Leroy Huizenga (2012, Oct. 4) when announcing that St Hildegard of Bingen would shortly be proclaimed a Doctor of the Church, refers to Hildegard's affinity with nature:

> Hildegard's vision of the cosmos and man's place therein is integral, seeing man as microcosm of the macrocosm, and so her prescription for various maladies often attempted to remedy imbalances caused by failure to live in harmony with nature. In this she is an antecedent of Pope Benedict's repeated call for an "ecology of man" that seeks to understand and promote the location of the human person in his rightful place within the ecology of nature, from which modern man is so severely estranged.

Flanagan (1998:92) notes that "Hildegard's idea of physiology is predicated upon her cosmology. The belief that man is constituted of the same (or similar) elements as those which constitute the world goes back to early Greek scientific speculation." Pope Benedict XVI referred to as the 'green pope' (William Patenaude, 2014) has written at length on 'preserving life on earth'. And now in his retirement the Pope Emeritus has recently published *The Garden of God: Toward a Human Ecology* (2014) whereby he writes that "man [humankind] if he/[she] is to have a heart for peace, must have an awareness of the connection between natural ecology and human ecology." The incumbent Pope Francis has also recently published a papal encyclical on the environment, *LAUDATO SI' On Care For Our Common Home* and this encyclical is a 'call to action' to the global community to accept responsibility to care for "Our Common Home" (Pope Francis, 2015, May 24).

Leaders and followers within the global community share in the responsibility to care for the world. Hildegard took her leadership responsibilities seriously for she didn't just serve her sisters in religion and the public. She served creation. Sims (1997:145) wisely advocates that stewardship should encompass more than just the 'trappings' of leadership, and that servant leaders should endeavour to serve creation: "[We should] seize our vocation of stewardship of the earth as a divine calling, that we learn to care for creation as servant leaders." Sims (1997:145) is advocating that "servant leaders are the custodians of nature, and are therefore stewards of the sacredness of life" (cited in Cameron, 2012).

Stewardship promotes leaders as agents of change. According to Boyd (2012:1) "Just as ecology deals with the relationship of organisms among themselves and to their physical environment, contemporary leadership can be viewed as an ecological system involving the interaction of humans with each other and their more complex environment." In this way leaders who promote stewardship will have a cosmic vision and engage in transformative action to mentor and nurture, to facilitate and utilise the talents and gifts of others by empowering them to be the best they can be in their service of stewardship to the global community (cited in Cameron, 2014).

The trilogy of visionary works of Hildegard are her legacy to humanity and with her other works referred to in the Criterion on her *Eminent Doctrine* in Chapter 4, have been held in trust by the members of the Benedictine Order since Hildegard's death in the twelfth century. Thus preserved and safeguarded for over eight hundred years the charism and message of Hildegard lives on in the twenty-first century. Peter Block (1996:xx) defines stewardship as holding something "in trust for another." According to Greenleaf (cited in Frick and Spears, 1996:353) "Not every institution or organisation, however, will have trustees to safeguard the inherent resources, so it is the responsibility of the leaders and followers of these groups, to accept accountability for their actions" and protect the resources entrusted to their care so that future generations will reap the benefits.

Hildegard's legacy has contributed significantly to the building of the Church community. Her 'equivalent canonisation' and elevation to the doctoral ranks in 2012 show, that she has the confidence of the Church.

14

COMMITMENT TO THE GROWTH OF PEOPLE

A servant leader is committed to making a difference in the lives of people and bringing out their magnificence by assisting them to achieve their goals (Blanchard, 2007:250). Spears (2010:29) emphasises that the servant leader, "is deeply committed to the growth of each and every individual within his or her organisation." Blanchard (2007:261) "maintains that it is the leaders who are called, who are willing to bring out the best in others: 'Since they believe their role in life is to serve, not to be served ... they thrive on developing others and the belief that individuals with expertise will come forward as needed throughout the organization.'"

Servant leadership is not just concerned with the growth of those being served but also with the growth of the leader. Ongoing experience in leadership situations and good mentoring from more experienced colleagues will often provide a leader with the necessary skills to grow (Hunter, 2004:41). Greenleaf (cited in Fraker and Spears, 1996:90; cited in Cameron, 2012:35) refers to the, "circular process ... the person builds the team and the team builds the person ... continuous interaction between persons and teams so that each nourishes the other." For Greenleaf this process results in strong teams of people interacting with each other and nourishing each other.

Hildegard demonstrated her commitment to the growth of people, through developing the spiritual growth of herself and her sisters in religion, through her understanding of the needs of others, by nurturing and empowering those in her care and by giving witness to the mandate given to her by the living Light "Speak therefore of these wonders, and, being so taught, write them and speak" (*Scivias*, 1990:59).

In his Apostolic Letter Proclaiming St Hildegard of Bingen a *Doctor of the Universal Church* Pope Benedict XVI refers to Hildegard's spirituality "At the basis of her spirituality was the Benedictine Rule which views spiritual balance and ascetical moderation as paths to holiness" (2012a:1). Newman writes that when Hildegard was placed in Jutta's care as a child "She learned to read the Latin Bible, particularly the psalms, and to chant the monastic Office" (1990:11). In Chapter 2 there is reference to Hildegard's explanation in receiving a limited education because it was being taught by an *unlearned woman* – *Jutta* (Flanagan, 1995) and it was not until the visionary experience of her *Spiritual Awakening* (see Chapter 9) that she received "infused knowledge of all the books of Scripture" (Newman, 1990:12).

Hildegard would have been in her early forties when this knowledge was revealed to her and she was able to influence many with her writing the source of which was divine revelation. Pope Benedict maintains that this influence was widespread: "The profound spirituality of her writings had a significant influence both on the faithful and on important figures of her time and brought about an incisive renewal of theology, liturgy, natural sciences and music" (2012a:2).

Benedict emphasises that Hildegard was committed to caring for the spiritual and physical 'well-being' of the members of her community: "Within the walls of the cloister, she cared for the spiritual and material well-being of her sisters, fostering in a special way community life, culture and the liturgy" (2012:1). Spears maintains that the "servant leader recognises the tremendous responsibility to do everything within his or her power to nurture the personal, professional, and spiritual growth of employees" (1998:6; cited in Cameron, 2012).

You may recall in Chapter 2 Jutta and Hildegard and another companion (also called Jutta) were enclosed as anchoresses at the monastery at Disibodenberg. However before long, "the fame of Jutta and her pupil [Hildegard] attracted other aspirants to the community" (Flanagan, 1998:36). As a result the small Benedictine community of nuns began to grow and an increasing number of "entrants ... were admitted [to the convent], rather than enclosed as anchoresses" (ibid.). The growing community of nuns followed the 'Benedictine Rule' (Newman, 1990:11). Flanagan posits that "Disibodenberg ... was not intended as a double monastery, [and] it is difficult to ascertain how things were arranged to accommodate both monks and nuns" (1998:37).

When Hildegard was elected to the position of prioress following the death of Jutta in 1136 she assumed the responsibility of caring for the "spiritual and material well-being" of her sisters in religion (Silvas, 1998). Their needs were her priority. When quoting from Hildegard's *Vita* (Life) Silvas refers to the discernment and patience displayed by Hildegard when dealing with members of her community who were prone to 'rebel'; for example "When there were rebels in the community she did not immediately reproach them sharply or cut them off. Instead she used to overlook, warn, put up with, and patiently bide the time, until through a revelation from God she received counsel as to what she should do about them" (1998:113).

When conditions became cramped because of the growing numbers, and about the time of the Synod of Bishops at Trier, Hildegard "received a vision in which she was instructed to leave Disibodenberg" (Newman, 1990:13). It was time for Hildegard to embark on her public life:

> [After] the culminating approval of Pope Eugene [of her writings] ... Hildegard felt strong enough to assert with prophetic vigour ...[that] her female community needed to move out of its cramped quarters to somewhere more

spacious where they might be free to develop as a distinct community. It would be difficult to overstate the sheer difficulties involved in this break with the monks of Disibodenberg: the legal wrangles, the financial worries, the barrage of criticism and so forth. But Hildegard resolutely pushed it through. The nuns moved to a new purpose-built monastery, down the Nahe on the left bank of its junction with the Rhine, at a place called Rupertsberg. The church [St Rupert] was consecrated on 1 May 1151 (Silvas, 2012:9).

Matthew and Gil Fairholm (2000:103) argue that leader effectiveness is "Correlated with people's trust in that leader … [trust is] the foundation of the philosophy of leadership … and is … essential in [developing positive] interpersonal relationships." You may recall there was much negativity by the community of monks at Disibodenberg when hearing that the nuns were keen to move and relocate to Mount St Rupert "*some thirty kilometers distant*" (Baird, 2006:29). Silvas recounts from Hildegard's *Vita* (Life): "Now when my Abbot and the brothers … realized the nature of the proposed change, that we were wanting to go from a lushness of fields and vineyards and from the beauty of that place to an arid place with no conveniences, they were shocked, and conspired among themselves to block us so that it should not come about" (1998:163).

However following approval from the Archbishop of Mainz and with Hildegard's health significantly improved (her health had again become precarious until formal permission was granted for the nun's departure) the nuns set off. Silvas comments on Hildegard's initial impression on their arrival at their destination: "When I began to dwell in that place with twenty noble women of wealthy parents, we found no dwelling or inhabitants there except for an ex-soldier and his wife and children … [though in time] many who at first jeered at us … came to us from all sides offering us help and filling us with blessings" (1998:165).

The sisters who accompanied Hildegard trusted that she had their best interests at heart. Their relocation was not easy "many of the nuns ... were loath to leave their comfortable surroundings for a desolate wilderness" (Newman, 1990:13). Remember the women were from noble families and coming from wealthy backgrounds few had experienced discomforts during their life-time (Degler, 2007:8-9). Interestingly Flanagan notes Hildegard's custom to accept only nobly born women into the Order:

> Hildegard once defended her practice of permitting only the daughters of the nobility to enter her convent by asking rhetorically whether a farmer would put his oxen, asses, sheep, and goats in the same stable... [for] what would ensue if people were treated in the same way, with the higher rank besetting the lower and the lower mounting above the higher (1998:211).

Remember Hildegard herself was from a noble family and she would have had a predilection for class distinction as highlighted in the quotation. The wealthy families were able to support the community of nuns and poorer families would have been unable to do this (however you will notice in the next chapter that with her second foundation at Eibingen Hildegard provided for the daughters of the poorer families to be able to join the order and serve in this convent).

After Hildegard and her sisters had left Disibodenberg and arrived at their destination "She nurtured the virgin nuns committed to her charge with motherly affection, and never ceased to instruct them wisely in the rules of the order" (Taken from the First Book of the life of the Virgin Saint Hildegard, cited in Silvas, 1998:147). Hildegard took her leadership responsibilities seriously and nurtured and mentored her sisters in religion. According to Benedict "there are 58 sermons, addressed directly to her sisters. They are her *Expositiones Evangeliorum*, containing a literary and moral commentary on Gospel passages related to the main celebrations of the liturgical year" (2012a:2).

Greenleaf's advice for a leader is to be a "servant first … make sure that other people's highest priority needs are being served" (1977:13). Greenleaf maintains that this approach can be tested by asking the following: "Do those served grow as persons? Do they, while being served, become healthier, wiser, freer, more autonomous more likely themselves to become servants?" (1977:13-14). Russell quotes Spears (1998) that, "'Commitment to the growth of people' is one of the critical characteristics of servant leadership" (2001:80). The following is an extract of a letter from Hildegard to the nuns of her community in their monastery at Rupertsberg:

> O daughters, you who have followed in Christ's footsteps [cf.1 Pet 2.21] in your love for chastity, and who have chosen me, poor little woman that I am, as a mother for yourselves – a choice made in the humility of obedience in order to exalt God – I say these things not on my own accord but according to a divine revelation speaking through my motherly affection for you. I have found this monastery – this resting place of the relics of St. Rupert the confessor, to whose refuge you have fled – resplendent with miracles, by God's will, offering up a sacrifice of praise [cf Ps 49.14]. I came to this place with the permission of my superiors and with God's assistance I gladly made it a home for myself and my followers (Baird, 2006:35-37).

The love, care and affection Hildegard has for her sisters are all evident in her words to them. They have chosen to follow her and serve God at the monastery of St Rupert. However Hildegard offers advice to those she leads:

> O Daughters of God, I admonish you to love one another, just as from my youth I, your mother, have admonished you, so that in this good will you might be a bright light with

the angels, and strong in your spirits, just as Benedict, your father, instructed you. May the Holy Spirit send you His gifts, because after my death you will no longer hear my voice. But never forget the sound of my voice among you, for it has so often resounded in love among you (Baird, 2006:37).

Hildegard is emphasising to her sisters that they must continue to share and serve her vision even when she is no longer with them. She values their strength and their spiritual gifts. She has taught them well. "The way you serve the vision is by developing people so that they can work on that vision even when you're not around" (Blanchard and Hodges, 2003:68). Hildegard had confidence in her nuns and their abilities. She respected and trusted them. Hunter (2004:98) emphasises the importance of giving respect and building trust, by recognising that others have abilities and skills and if they are delegated responsibilities in line with their capabilities, they will grow and develop, and if given the opportunity they will become leaders themselves. Drucker (cited in Hunter, 2004:123-124) stresses the importance of trust to a leader: "the final requirement of effective leadership is to earn trust. Otherwise there won't be any followers – and the only definition of a leader is someone who has followers."

As mentor and nurturer of the sisters entrusted to her care Hildegard guided them and on occasion she was criticised by others for her seemingly 'unorthodox' leadership practices. Baird refers to a letter sent to Hildegard by a Mistress Tengswich and maintains that the letter *"can only be described as a mordant personal attack on Hildegard ...* [It is well] *written in a style suffused with irony that verges at times on sarcasm, the letter gives a graphic and deliciously detailed description of the goings-on, so offensive to Tengswich's pietistic tastes, in that, as she saw it, all-too-liberal community"* (2006:24-26).

> To Hildegard, mistress of the brides of Christ, Tengswich, unworthy superior of the sisters at Andernach, with a prayer

that she eventually be joined to the highest order of spirits in heaven. The report of your saintliness has flown far and wide and has brought to our attention things wondrous and remarkable … We have learned from a number of people that an angel from above reveals many secrets of heaven for you to record, difficult as they are for mortal minds to grasp, as well as some things that you are to do, not in accordance with human wisdom, but as God himself instructs them to be done.

We have, however, also heard about certain strange and irregular practices that you countenance. They say that on feast days your virgins stand in the church with unbound hair when singing the psalms and that as part of their dress they wear white, silk veils, so long that they touch the floor. Moreover, it is said that they wear crowns of gold filigree into which are inserted crosses on both sides and the back, with a figure of the Lamb on the front, and that they adorn their fingers with golden rings. And all this despite the express prohibition of the great shepherd of the Church, who writes in admonition: Let women comport themselves with modesty "not with plaited hair, or gold, or pearls, or costly attire" [I Tim 2.9].

Moreover, that which seems no less strange to us is the fact that you admit into your community only those women from noble, well-established families and absolutely reject others who are of lower birth and of less wealth … O worthy bride of Christ, such unheard-of practices far exceed the capacity of our weak understanding … Therefore, we have decided to send this humble little letter to you, saintly lady, asking by whose authority you can defend such practices (ibid.).

Surprisingly Baird maintains that Hildegard did not retaliate with words of denial or recrimination but does however mount *"an elaborate argument to justify her practices"* (2006:26):

To Mistress Tengswich

The Living Fountain says: Let a woman remain within her chamber so that she may preserve her modesty, for the serpent breathed the fiery danger of horrible lust into her ... O, woman, what a splendid being you are! For you have set your foundation in the sun, and have conquered the world ... a woman, once married, ought not to indulge herself in prideful adornment of hair or person, nor ought she to lift herself in prideful adornment of hair or person, nor ought she to lift herself up to vanity, wearing a crown and other golden ornaments, except at her husband's pleasure, and even then with moderation.

But these strictures do not apply to a virgin, for she stands in the unsullied purity of paradise, lovely and unwithering, and she always remains in the full vitality of the budding rod. A virgin is not commanded to cover up her hair, but she willingly does so out of her great humility, for a person will naturally hide the beauty of her soul, lest, on account of her pride, the hawk carry it off.

Virgins are married with holiness in the Holy Spirit and in the bright dawn of virginity, and so it is proper that they come before the great High priest as an oblation presented to God. Thus through the permission granted her and the revelation of the mystic inspiration of the finger of God, it is appropriate for a virgin to wear a white vestment, the lucent symbol of her betrothal to Christ.

Hildegard then responds to the allegation by Tengswich of her acceptance into the order of only women who are nobly born and from wealthy families (discussed in an earlier paragraph in this chapter):

> God also keeps a watchful eye on every person, so that a lower order will not gain ascendancy over a higher one, as Satan and the first man did ... it is clear that differentiation

must be maintained in these matters, lest people of varying status, herded all together, be dispersed through the pride of their elevation, on the one hand, or the disgrace of their decline on the other ... For God establishes ranks on earth, just as in heaven with angels, archangels, thrones, dominions, cherubim, and seraphim. And they are all loved by God, although they are not equal in rank ... God has infused human beings with good understanding so that their name will not be destroyed.

These words do not come from a human being but from the Living Light ... (cited in Baird, 2006:28-29).

This consciousness of class distinction did not seem to be a problem for Hildegard who was nobly born and thus would have been accustomed to the ways and thinking of the nobility.

People need to be motivated. Greenleaf (1977:145) maintains that "motivation ... becomes what people generate for themselves when they experience growth." When people are suitably motivated they work together as a team, "being effective in today's organizations is a team game, and without collaboration and teamwork skills, you are unlikely to be successful" (Blanchard, 2007:167). In Chapter 4 there is reference to a 'secret language' invented by Hildegard. Newman refers to this as "the mysterious *Lingua ignota*, which she seems to have created as a kind of secret language to instil a sense of mystical solidarity among her nuns" (1990:13).

Benedict refers to the 'linguistic writings' "as the *Lingua Ignota* [Unknown Language] and the *Litterae Ignotae* [Unknown Writing], in which the words appear in an unknown language of her own invention, but are composed mainly of phonemes present in German" (2012a:2). You may recall that Flanagan (1995) notes that the unknown language "is a glossary of some nine hundred invented words (mostly nouns) thematically arranged. They include the names of plants and herbs and so may have been related to Hildegard's scientific interest.

Although the invented alphabet is used occasionally for titles in her correspondence, her only use of the unknown language occurs in the *Symphonia*" (p. 4).

Regarding the *Symphonia* Newman maintains that "To instruct her nuns she wrote a commentary on the Athanasian creed, and she [also] enriched their liturgical life with the repertoire of songs that she eventually gathered into her *Symphonica*" (1990:13). The *Symphonica* or *Symphonia* is in reference to Hildegard's music which she combined "into a cycle called The Symphony of the Harmony of the Heavenly Revelations. This title refers not only to the heavenly inspiration of her music but to the place music held in her schema as the highest form of praise to God" (Nancy Fierro, 1997:1-2).

Pope Benedict XVI at the second of the General Audiences on Hildegard (8 September, 2010b) also makes mention of "other writings [where] Hildegard manifests the versatility of interests and cultural vivacity of the female monasteries of the Middle Ages, in a manner contrary to the prejudices which still weighed on that period" (2010b:3). So about the time of the invention of the 'secret language' during the 1150s (Newman, 1990:13) Hildegard also wrote the 'Play of Virtues' (*Ordo Virtutum*).

Butcher (2013:69) states that *The Play of Virtues* is a medieval musical drama and "a splendid staging of the Soul's struggle with the Devil. It is also the earliest surviving morality play." The play narrates a struggle between virtues and the devil for possession of a human soul. Butcher (2013:72) claims that Hildegard encouraged some of her Rupertsberg nuns to "sing the roles of the seventeen Virtues, the Soul, and the group of lamenting souls" Apparently the one male role, that of the devil which was not a singing role because the devil "has divorced himself from all heavenly harmony … [and] shouts his way through the work" (ibid.) may have been given to the monk Volmar, Hildegard's secretary and spiritual adviser. The play is about choices and would have been a good lesson for the nun's in their interaction with one another for "Life is all about the choices we make as we interact with each other. [As leaders] we can choose to be self-serving or serving" (Blanchard, 2007:76).

Hildegard's influence did not just extend beyond the boundaries of her two monasteries her influence transcends the centuries. In the words of Pope Benedict XVI in 2010, "this great woman, this 'prophetess' … speaks with great timeliness to us today" (2010b:2). Let us listen and let us learn!

15

BUILDING COMMUNITY

Greenleaf referred to Jesus Christ as the "great leader builder" (1977:140-144) and as "the Son of Man [he] did not come to be served, but to serve" [Matthew 20:28]. Anzalone maintains "The community that the servant leader builds is a team that works synergistically since the true servant leader is interested in developing leaders and does not hoard decision making" (2007:803). In other words as DeGraaf et al. (2001:23) emphasise "A community is a sum of its parts, so a good community must be made up of virtuous citizens" working together collaboratively.

Taulbert (2008:36) defines building community as a "dynamic process that connects leadership to those who follow. Leadership and followership are one coin with two sides – they are interdependent and essential for each other's success. Effective leaders create and support an environment that lends itself to productive followership." Taulbert states further, that it is in the best interest of all concerned in the organisation, if the leader takes the time to build community for he emphasises that the most valued resource in the community, is its people (ibid.). Hunter (2004:207) stresses the importance of building community to create a healthy environment in which people can live and work free of unnecessary barriers and distractions. Hildegard demonstrated building community through living in a community and following the Benedictine Rule, through building up the community of the Church by her efforts at reform, through her apostolic, pastoral activity, and through establishing two monasteries during her lifetime.

"The Church is one model of a serving institution which can nurture spirituality and be a positive influence in the lives of the members, who in turn could then reach out to others thus encouraging spiritual and physical growth" (Greenleaf, cited in Fraker and Spears, 1996:55). Remember in Chapter 2 it was in the environment of a church community at Disibodenberg that Hildegard grew from childhood to adulthood. She had come from a large family of ten children to a religious community (Newman, 1990:11). Admittedly in those early years in the anchorhold, companionship was restricted to just a few (Blessed Jutta, Hildegard and another by the name of Jutta) but they were still a part of the community at Disibodenberg. And then about 1150 due in part to the increasing growth in the numbers of young women entering the order Hildegard by now prioress and leader of her community (Silvas, 2012:8) relocated a group of her nuns to Rupertsberg thus establishing her first monastery which was consecrated in 1152. Hildegard's foundation required foresight and planning. According to Silvas:

> So that it might not seem that she had taken over and occupied what properly belonged to another, she secured her new abode from its former owners partly by purchase and partly by an exchange of property, using the offerings of the faithful which the fame of her reputation had attracted. Once she had obtained it freehold, she made sure it would always remain freehold; since it was subject to the protection of the church of Mainz, [and] she would have no other defender than one from the Bishop's See itself (1998:147).

Here Hildegard is ensuring that the property will always belong to the nuns and she is negotiating in the best interests of the members of her community. She opted to receive advice from a member of the Bishop's See rather than trust a "lay advocate" (ibid.) who might not put the interests of Hildegard and her community first. As to the nuns spiritual needs a decision was made to come to some agreement with the monks at Disibodenberg (Silvas, 1998:147).

As circumstances and times required it, they would receive priests from the monastery whom they themselves had asked for by name according to their individual and free choice. These were to support them as much through the care of souls and the celebration of the holy liturgy as through the administration of temporal goods. The venerable Henry and Arnold, Metropolitans of Mainz not only gave their permission and counsel to these provisions but decreed and ratified them in writing with the consent of abbots, so that by the authority of privileges the community of St Disibod was precluded from usurping a right over the estates of St Rupert, or to put it more accurately was forbidden to do so by the Divine power on high (ibid.).

Now Hildegard realised that she would have to return to her former monastery to discuss the negotiations but "hung back at first through alarm … [however] she was struck by the whip of divine reproof and became sick almost to the point of death" (Silvas, 1998:148). It was only when Hildegard decided to do what God was ordering her to do that she felt well enough to persevere with the task. "She then asked that she be placed on a horse and supported by hands be led off. As soon as she had been led a very little way along the road she recovered her strength and went gladly on her way" (ibid.).

The monks at the monastery at Disibodenberg had never really come to terms with Hildegard's departure from the monastery with her group of nuns. In a letter to Hildegard, Adelbert, Prior at Mount St. Disibod (referred elsewhere in this book as Disibodenberg) informs Hildegard that they have accepted her decision but questions the reasons for God's action in this matter:

> [W]e (who have known you almost from the cradle and with whom you lived for many years) wonder why you have withdrawn the words of your celestial visions from us who thirst for them.

> We remember how you were educated among us, how you were taught, how you were established in the religious life. For your instruction was that appropriate only to a woman, and a simple psalter was your only schoolbook. Yet without complaint you embraced the good and holy religious life. But the will of God filled you with celestial dew … and opened up to you the magnitude of its secrets. And just as we were set to rejoice in these things with you, God took you away from us against our will, and gave you to other people. We cannot fathom why God did this … (Baird, 2006:31).

Hildegard's reluctance initially to set out for Disibodenberg suggests that perhaps some conflict still existed between the two communities however by deciding to travel to Disibodenberg to discuss the negotiations she was recognising the value of conflict resolution for a healthy positive relationship between the two communities. Hunter (2004:208) emphasises that "Community is not a place free from conflict. Indeed, when two or more people are gathered together for a purpose, there will be conflict – at least there should be in a healthy community ... [for a] community is a place not of conflict avoidance but of conflict resolution." On her arrival at Disibodenberg Hildegard:

> explained why she was compelled to come, and, while there, separated the place of her new monastery along with some other properties belonging to her community from the brothers of that monastery, but left to them the larger portion of possessions which had been given to it when the sisters had been first received, and in addition left them a not inconsiderable sum of money so that there might remain no just cause for complaint (Silvas, 1998:148-149).

As mentioned this was an effort on Hildegard's part at conflict resolution though obviously these terms would not be familiar to a leader in the twelfth century. It seems as if she was trying to settle an argument amicably to at least maintain some semblance of a relationship between the two communities. Newman (1990:13-14) notes that from the time of her arrival at Rupertsberg Hildegard did all that she could to secure "the welfare of her monastery ... She worked to establish monastic discipline by teaching and preaching; supervised construction of the new buildings; obtained gifts and bequests to make her community financially secure ... [and] fought for a charter of independence from St. Disibod..."

During this time Hildegard completed the first in her trilogy of visionary works the *Scivias*. According to information in the book of her life (*Vita*):

> Once the Blessed Virgin had moved to that place to which she had been divinely ordered, she finished the book of her visions which she had begun at Disibodenberg. Moved by the spirit of prophecy, she also composed certain books on the nature of man, the elements and the variety of created things, and how human beings might derive help from this knowledge and many other secrets (Silvas, 1998:155).

Newman emphasises that "This intense burst of activity directed toward [her work and] her daughters was complemented by an ever-widening correspondence with the outside world. Hildegard's growing fame brought a constant stream of pilgrims and miracle-seekers as well as prospective nuns, to the Rupertsberg gates" (1990:13-14). Hildegard was building community. She was contributing to the growth in numbers of the nuns in her community as her fame and reputation spread throughout the land. Taulbert maintains (2008) that building community is all about building people.

Remember in Chapter 2 that Bermersheim is given as the birth place of Hildegard. Sister Teresa Tromberend a Benedictine nun has written an article on Bermersheim in which she provides data authenticating 'Bermersheim' as the birthplace of Hildegard. Apparently the convent at Rupertsberg received donations from the region known as the birthplace of Hildegard. This source of financial assistance would have been welcome for the growing community. "It is a striking fact, that the catalogue of goods (foundation book) of the convent of Rupertsberg, founded by Hildegard around 1150, at the top of all entries on nine pages registers donations from the region of Bermersheim" (Tromberend, 1996:1-2).

It would seem that though Hildegard came from a large family she was the youngest and around 1158 when Hildegard was about 60 years old "a deed of donation … confirms the donation of the manor house of Bermersheim and other estates to the 'Ladies' of the Rupertsberg convent." Additional assistance for the fledgling community at Rupertsberg, Hildegard's first foundation was also provided for by "*a local noblewoman, the Margravine Richardis von Stade, mother of one of her nuns* [remember Richardis], *and by Heinrich, Archbishop of the Diocese*" (Baird, 2006:29).

Interestingly during the historical research regarding Hildegard's foundations it is apparent that the titles 'convent' and 'monastery' are used interchangeably. For example in an article on 'The Rupertsberg' a Dr Josef Krasenbrink (1996:1) writes "Between 1147 and 1151, Hildegard left the Disibodenberg and founded her first monastery above the tomb of St. Rupertus. Her biography recounts: 'Hildegard was shown by the Holy Spirit that place where the Nahe flows into the Rhine namely the hill which received its name by the confessor St. Rupertus.'" And then Krasenbrink cites a description of the convent by Wibert of Gembloux (Guibert) in about 1177:

> this convent has not been founded by an emperor or bishop, a mighty or a rich man of this world, but by a poor and weak woman, a newcomer in this region. Within a short time, only 27 years, the monastic spirit and the outside construction have developed to such high standards, that not by magnificent but well-built and spacious buildings it is in an excellent condition (ibid.).

You may recall when Volmar, Hildegard's secretary and confidant died in 1173 he was replaced by Godfrey who died in 1176 and it was Guibert who replaced Godfrey (Silvas, 1998:xxi). Sims (1997:68-70) refers to the influence of the spirit in building community and maintains that the spirit reconnects, "The human soul is reconnected to one's larger self, immersed and fulfilled in the experience of community ... the ... great work of the spirit is the building and restoring of community." Guibert in the above quotation writes about 'the monastic spirit' in reference to Hildegard's foundation and Krasenbrink (1996:1) maintains "The spiritual radiation of the Rupertsberg ceased when Hildegard died in 1179." Apparently the monastery was destroyed in 1632 and never rebuilt (ibid.).

In her notes from the book of the life of Hildegard, Silvas writes about the second foundation at Eibingen:

> In 1165 [at about the age of 67 years] Hildegard founded a second monastery of nuns just across the Rhine at Eibingen, using the remains of an Augustinian double foundation destroyed by Emperor Frederick ... Here she settled her nuns who were not nobly born, and twice a week used to visit them. Thus she could be readily found by those seeking her help while she was travelling between the two houses. Eibingen still flourishes today as the Benediktinerinnenabtei St Hildegard (1998:192).

One of the reasons for the acquisition of a second foundation was due to the growing numbers in her community which is a testament to the good works being performed by Hildegard and her band of nuns. In his article on *The Old Convent of Eibingen* a Dr Werner Lauter provides more detail on Hildegard's second foundation.

> Hildegard of Bingen founded two monasteries: the Rupertsberg convent near Bingen and the Eibingen convent nor far from Rüdesheim. At Eibingen the noblewoman

Marka of Rüdesheim had founded an Augustinian double convent in 1148, which was already deserted in 1165 due to the chaos of war caused by the Emperor Barbarossa. The constant growing of the Rupertsberg convent led Hildegard to acquire the damaged buildings in 1165. She had them restored for thirty Benedictine sisters and henceforth crossed the Rhine twice a week from the Rupertsberg to the new Eibingen community. In 1219, on April 22nd, about four decades after Hildegard's death, Pope Honorius III took the Eibingen convent under his protection … In 1632, during the Thirty Years' War, the Swedes destroyed the monastery of Rupertsberg by fire. Via Cologne the nuns arrived at the Eibingen monastery with the relics of St. Hildegard in 1636, where they suffered from poverty and privation. The plundering by mercenary troops gave cause for their later flight to Mainz. The sisters could only return at the end of 1641 (Lauter, 1996:1).

Building projects and renovations were carried out over the years with the church and the west wing fully restored during the years 1681 to 1683. Pope Clemens XI wrote a letter in 1701, dedicating the church to St. Rupert and St. Hildegard. According to Lauter (1996:2) "In 1709, a small prayer book was printed by the publisher Johann Mayren of Mainz, initiated by the Eibingen convent, saying: 'Register of the most noble relics … So kept in the virgin convent of high nobility in Eibingen in the Rhine Province, respectfully preserved …'" Sr Philippa Rath (1996:1) a Benedictine nun maintains that a "new Abbey of St Hildegard of Eibingen was built a little up the hill above the old monastery" during the years 1900 to 1904.

However Lauter (1996:1) in an article on *Hildegardis Reliquary in the Eibingen Parish Church* maintains that there was a fire in the Eibingen church some three centuries after the fire that destroyed the Rupertsberg monastery and that even though the fire in 1932 was severe with the church and part of the building destroyed "the Hildegardis reliquary

... [was] saved". Lauter notes that on the anniversary of the death of Hildegard on 17 September each year "an increasing number of pilgrims come to Eibingen every year to join the procession of relics in honour of the great Saint" (ibid.).

Rath (1996:1) in her article above refers to the Rule of St Benedict as being "over 1400 years old" with its emphasis on "life in a community. Divine service and liturgy are the centre of monastic life. Since 'nothing should be given preference over the work of God'" (ibid.). Hildegard and her nuns lived the community life well and the evidence is its growth. Blanchard (2007:xxiii) quotes Shula: "If you don't shoot for excellence, you never have a chance of getting there." It is everybody working together as a team in the organisation that will ensure that there is a standard of excellence and that the desired goals are achieved (cited in Cameron, 2012).

Earlier in this chapter we referred to the monk Guibert of Gembloux. In her work on the Book of Life (*Vita*) of Hildegard, Silvas notes that "Guibert (or Wibert) was born in Brabant and attended the monastery school at Gembloux, where he achieved a very high standard of Latin literacy. There he became a monk and priest. He lived at Rupertsberg from 1177 to 1180 remaining there for a year after Hildegard's death" when he was recalled to Gembloux (1998:89).

Now Baird (2006:135) refers to a letter written to Hildegard in 1175 when Hildegard was about 77 years of age. The letter was from Guibert "*who was to become her last intimate associate and secretary*":

> *Having read her works and having reflected, as he says, upon the gifts bestowed upon her by the Holy Spirit ... he writes in burning curiosity, seeking answers to certain questions he has about her divine inspiration: Does she give voice to her visions in German while someone else takes them down in Latin? Does she, 'as is commonly said', forget her visions as soon as they are written down? Is she learned, or does her wisdom come wholly through inspiration? When Hildegard failed to answer this*

> *first letter, he wrote again, adding further questions: Does she receive her visions in dreams while asleep, or do they come in a state of ecstasy? Are her nuns' crowns dictated by divine inspiration, or are they merely for feminine ornamentation? Does the title of her book Scivias mean 'Knowing the Ways', or is there a better translation? Has she written any other books ... He was to write her in all some eight long ... letters.*

As the provost and private secretary to Hildegard it might be assumed that Guibert would know the answers to most of the questions he puts to Hildegard in his correspondence to her. Eventually Hildegard responds and though all the questions are not answered Baird (2006:136) emphasises that *"the letter is very informative, giving details that we get nowhere else. Although, for instance, Hildegard refers constantly to the Living light in all her writing, here, for the first and only time, we hear of a Shadow of the Living Light."*

Some of Hildegard's response to Guibert:

> I am now more than seventy years old. But even in my infancy, before my bones, muscles, and veins had reached their full strength, I was possessed of this visionary gift in my soul, and it abides with me still up to the present day ... The light that I see is not local and confined ... This light I have named "the shadow of the Living Light" ... And my seeing, hearing, and knowing are simultaneous, so that I learn and know at the same instant. But I have no knowledge of anything I do not see there, because I am unlearned. Thus the things I write are those that I see and hear in my vision, with no words of my own added. And these are expressed in unpolished Latin, for that is the way I hear them in my vision, since I am not taught in the vision to write the way philosophers do ... In a vision I also saw that my first book of visions was to be called *Scivias*, for it was brought forth by way of the Living Light ... I also had a vision about crowns (cited in Baird, 2006:138-140).

Hildegard then describes in detail the crown that her nuns now wore and what she saw in her vision including "a circlet of three colours joined into one" (ibid.) with the circlet representing the Holy Trinity. Guibert is thrilled with Hildegard's response and his words of praise are profuse in his reply.

Silvas (1998:90) maintains that "Guibert's letters are a quarry of historical and biographical information about Hildegard and her network of supporters and friends." We are told that it is in a letter to a Radulf of Villers that Guibert has the most to tell about Hildegard and in his letters he also tells "how he came to know Hildegard and stay at her monastery and also [refers] to the friendship between her and Archbishop Philip von Heinsberg of Cologne. It is from his correspondence we learn the name of Hildegard's collaborator, Volmar" (ibid.).

Hildegard's contribution to the growth of the Church community was outstanding. The following emphasises that Hildegard's written contributions, her musical compositions, her healing 'gifts' and her teaching all promoted her 'genius' in assisting the Church in its mission:

> The prodigious genius of Hildegard poured itself out in the second half of her life in a flurry of literary work, musical compositions, and pastoral activity. She was known as a wonder-worker, and there are many interesting tales of her healings in her *Vitae* and the *Acta Inquisitionis*, precious vignettes into the social life of the times. She had a special gift for dispelling demons and curing mental illnesses ... Between 1158 and 1177 she undertook four major preaching tours, visiting not only many monasteries where she was much sought after, but even the Cathedral in Cologne where she had some ripe words to say to the clergy (Silvas, 2012:10).

Leaders like Hildegard are needed in the contemporary world who are not just content with the status quo, but who will challenge the 'establishment.' Greenleaf (1977:144) stresses the need for: "determined builders ... who can move creatively with these times in which powerful new forces for integrity are operating" (cited in Cameron, 2009). In his Apostolic Letter proclaiming St Hildegard a *Doctor of the Universal Church* Pope Benedict XVI emphasised that "One of the salient points of Hildegard's magisterium was her heartfelt exhortation to a virtuous life addressed to consecrated men and women ... Hildegard's eminent doctrine echoes the teaching of the Apostles, the Fathers and writings of her own day, while it finds a constant point of reference in the Rule of Saint Benedict" (2012a:5).

During the Homily at the Holy Mass for the opening of the Synod of Bishops and Proclamation of St John of Ávila and St Hildegard of Bingen as 'Doctors of the Church' Pope Benedict reinforces the words of Pope St John Paul II in 1979 when he described St Hildegard as a "Light for her people and her time" and not just for her time but a role model for women and men in the contemporary Church: "Saint Hildegard of Bingen, an important female figure of the twelfth century, offered her precious contribution to the growth of the Church of her time, employing the gifts received from God and showing herself to be a woman of brilliant intelligence deep sensitivity and recognised spiritual authority" (2012a:2). Here Benedict is praising Hildegard for contributing to the "growth of the Church of her time" – that is contributing to the building of the Church community during her own time and as Hildegard has been proclaimed a doctor of the Church in contemporary times that contribution now extends through the ages until 'time immemorial'.

Like St Hildegard "We are all leaders in some part of our lives" (Blanchard, 2007:278). People are responsible for building communities – in their homes, their schools, their workplaces, their churches, their businesses, their sporting institutions – and indeed, the list is endless (cited in Cameron, 2012). As Sims so eloquently expresses, all members of the human race are "part of a vast pulsating, interwoven web of life" (1997:134). Heider supports this concept: "Since all creation is a whole, separateness is an illusion. Like it or not, we are team players. [And] [p]ower comes through cooperation, independence through service, and a greater self through selflessness" (1985:77; cited in Cameron, 2009). Hence we all need to work together collaboratively with the *Spirit* in order to build (and if necessary restore) our communities!

PART THREE

A SNAPSHOT COMPARISON OF FOUR WOMEN & CONCLUSION

16

A Snapshot Comparison of Four Women

Introduction

To date (September 2015) there are thirty-six Doctors of the Universal Church – thirty-two males and four females (see Glossary for full list of names). The four female doctors comprise: St Hildegard of Bingen born in Germany at the end of the eleventh century and proclaimed a Doctor by Pope Benedict XVI on 7 October 2012; St Catherine of Siena born in Italy in the fourteenth century and proclaimed a Doctor by Blessed Pope Paul VI on 4 October 1970; St Teresa of Ávila born in Spain in the sixteenth century and proclaimed a Doctor by Blessed Pope Paul VI on 27 September 1970 and St Thérèse of Lisieux born in France in the nineteenth century and proclaimed a Doctor by Pope St John Paul II on 19 October 1997.

Hildegard, Catherine, Teresa, and Thérèse were all born in different centuries, countries and cultures and by virtue of their proclamation as doctors of the Church their teaching is relevant not just for their own times but 'for time immemorial.' Payne (2002:27; cited in Cameron, 2012) explains: "Their [doctors] theological contribution must have some lasting or permanent value ... [for according to Betti] candidates are meant to be 'doctors of the Church' not merely for their own times, but for all time."

In this book the ten core characteristics of servant leadership have been applied to the life and works of St Hildegard of Bingen. In

Leadership as a call to service: The lives and works of Teresa of Ávila, Catherine of Siena and Thérèse of Lisieux (2012) the ten core characteristics of servant leadership were applied to the lives and works of St Teresa of Ávila, St Catherine of Siena and St Thérèse of Lisieux (listed in the order in which they received their doctoral title).

The following presents a snapshot comparison of the four women doctors of the Catholic Church when the ten core characteristics of servant leadership are applied to their lives and works. Excerpts from the above 2012 book (pp. 217-243) on Catherine, Teresa and Thérèse have been used in the comparison and the information on Hildegard is taken from the relevant chapters within this book.

LISTENING

Hildegard

The visions of Hildegard were all seen with the 'inner eye' and heard with the 'inner ear' – she saw she listened and she responded. Hildegard asserted that all her visions were divinely inspired and were the result of inward revelation (Scivias, 1990:59-60). Such is reflective listening, which is a skill that "enables the listener to understand the content of the message as well as the feelings of the person who is speaking" (DeGraaf et al., 2001:4).

Hildegard possessed the skill of listening and this is demonstrated by her response to the 'inner voice' heard in the many visions she experienced. Listening to the inner voice, is described by John Gardiner (cited in Spears, 1998:116), as being attuned to a "'quiet presence,' ... [which is a place] 'where leadership and the Spirit meet.'"

Catherine

Catherine was in touch with her inner reality (Gardiner, cited in Spears, 1998:117) and responded to the voice of God in particular (Noffke,

1980). The silence of listening is evident in Catherine's life particularly during her ecstatic trances when she listened and responded to a higher power. Catherine recounted to her scribes what she heard from God while in ecstasy.

Catherine demonstrated the skill of listening, which she developed through the balance of what her body, mind and spirit communicated, as well as her openness to this communication, particularly during her mystic experiences and her active listening to those around her and to those in authority.

Teresa

During her lifetime Teresa was revered by some and criticised by others. Her literary work was prolific but always 'guarded' for she was ever mindful of the watchful eye of the Inquisition as it 'ruthlessly' implemented its policy on censorship (Ahlgren, 1996:15). Teresa's *Interior Castle* (Peers, 1963b) shows that she was proficient in the skill of "Listening to the internal voice … reflective listening" (DeGraaf et al., 2001:3-4). Teresa had developed the "power of active listening" (Brooks, 2006:12), in her interaction with confessors, religious nuns and priests, ecclesial and lay officials and members of the general public.

Teresa possessed the skill of listening, which she developed through her knowledge of self (listening to the inner voice), listening to others (those involved in her foundations) and listening to God – Teresa credited God with her foundations.

Thérèse

Thérèse's skill of listening is evident when she becomes attuned to her inner voice, "I have never heard Jesus speak, but I feel he is within me. He guides me at every moment, and inspires me with the right thing to say or do" (O'Mahony, 1975:39). Thérèse's autobiography is her legacy to the Church, and is the product of her listening and responding to a request from her sister, Mother Agnes (Pauline) to write her autobiography – The *Story of a Soul* (Clarke, 1996).

Thérèse possessed the skill of listening, through listening to her sisters in religion when they requested small favours and, prior to her entry to Carmel, through her reflective listening to the inner voice, when she was determined to overcome any obstacles to achieve admittance to the Order.

Empathy

Hildegard

Degler (2007:9) reveals some of the emotional 'make-up' of this saint of Bingen: "Hildegard was not only compassionate, she was also a virtual firebrand when it came to issues of what we would call today social justice." "She wrote to kings, queens and popes, archbishops, abbesses and abbots, nuns and monks, laywomen and laymen, seeking advice and giving it, even when it was not sought" (Posa, 2012:1).

Hildegard's empathetic skills are evident through her concern and compassion for others particularly through her empathy and love for the Church, its members and her sisters in religion. Hildegard empathised with those with whom she came in contact offering advice and healing using her special gifts.

Catherine

Catherine had an innate presence that drew people to her and she empathised with them. Catherine's empathetic skills were prominent in her acceptance of humanity and in her efforts to meet the needs of those who sought her healing, care, counsel and compassion. She corresponded with people from all walks of life (Noffke, 2000, 2001, 2007 & 2008). Pope Gregory XI was a recipient of a number of letters from Catherine, for she empathised with the Church and its followers in their time of need. In Catherine's time factions were breaking out within the Papal States. Catherine also advised the Pope, who was residing in Avignon, to overcome his fear and his reliance on family and friends, and for the sake of the welfare of his people to return the papacy to Rome (Cameron, 2012:136-137).

Catherine demonstrated the skill of empathy through her inclusive nature, which embraced all in love and compassion.

Teresa

Teresa's concern for the needs of her nuns and their continued spiritual development in prayer enabled her to develop her empathetic skills which were further extended to include her desire to assist the Church in its 'hour' of need (Ahlgren, 1996:36). It was during the sixteenth century that protestors reacted to calls for reform and renewal by engaging in and establishing the religious movement which became known as the Reformation (Cameron, 2012:93). Teresa's charity, and her care and compassion for the sick and needy were qualities that received prominence in the testimonials given at the process for her canonisation (Peers, 1963c:339).

Teresa demonstrated empathy in the care and concern she showed for the Church, clergy and for her sisters in religion and for friends and members of the public involved in her foundations; however there were occasions when her forceful personality was tested by ecclesiastical and lay authorities.

Thérèse

Thérèse's empathetic skills were realised in her compassion towards the poor and the marginalised (O'Mahony, 1975:93; Clarke, 1996:99-100). In her dealings with her novices she was strict but kind, teaching her charges to be obedient and committed to the Rule (Jamart,

1961:84). She forgave those novices and superiors who were difficult and accepted their "treatment with humility" (O'Mahony, 1975:119). Hunter (2004:104) states "Forgiveness is an attribute of love." Thérèse guided her novices and those around her. When she entered Carmel Thérèse dedicated her life at her profession by pledging the following: "I came to save souls and especially to pray for priests" (Clarke, 1996:49).

Thérèse possessed the skill of empathy during her lifetime through her compassion and care for others and through empathetic listening to her novices. Since her death, many followers have empathised with Thérèse's teaching.

HEALING

Hildegard

Though she lived until the age of eighty-one Hildegard suffered continually from ill health and indeed on many occasions her suffering was so excruciating that her sisters in religion prepared for the worst, as her illness appeared to be life-threatening. Degler in her notes refers to the findings of some scholars and historians as regards to Hildegard's general health: *"It is generally accepted that Hildegard suffered from, among other things, severely debilitating migraines"* (2007:5). Hildegard authored works on medicine and natural sciences specifically she wrote on medicine and nature (natural philosophy and medicine) in the *Physica* and *Causae et Curae* which became her 'Classic Works on Health and Healing' (Throop, 1998).

Hildegard's healing skills were highly developed. Silvas (1998:181) quotes from the *Third Book on the Miracles of Saint Hildegard* which emphasises that "SO POWERFUL A CHARISM of healings shone out in the blessed virgin, that scarcely anyone approached her sick who did not immediately regain good health."

Catherine

Raymond (cited in Kearns, 1980) praises Catherine's healing powers particularly her many miracles to heal the mind, soul, and body of people she knew and those she did not know. Catherine was inclusive of the needs of all (Sims, 1997:87). In Raymond of Capua's biography of Catherine, Kearns relates Raymond's description of Catherine's mission: "as one of healing, enlightening and sanctifying and that "Catherine ... had been chosen and prepared by God, and sent to the world and the Church of her own time with power and authority to accomplish a divine mission in their regard" (1980:liii).

Catherine possessed the skill of healing and undertook the healing process for others, in light of her own infirmities. During her lifetime, she was credited with miraculous intercessions (Fink, 2000b:108), particularly during the outbreak of the plague in Siena.

Teresa

Heider (1985:55) quotes Lao Tzu on a leader as *A Warrior, a Healer and Tao*, "To lead is to act with power and decision whilst also acting as a 'healer ... in an open, receptive and nourishing state.'" Teresa suffered chronic ill-health for most of her life (Fink, 2000b:124). In spite of her 'ailments' Teresa accomplished 'great things' – healing self and others (Peers, 1963a, 1963b). Her niece, Sister Teresa de Jesús, in her testimony given in 1596, states that Teresa suffered greatly when making her foundations: "[S]he suffered great trials and inconveniences, and was often ill, but this never sufficed to deter her from what she had begun, nor would she postpone a journey by so much as a day" (Peers, 1963c:366). During Teresa's early years in the convent her spiritual health also was an issue of concern (Cameron, 2012:97).

Teresa possessed the skill of healing, with the healing process tending initially to focus on her personal healing, prior to reaching out to transform and "make whole" the lives of others.

Thérèse

During her short life Thérèse experienced a gamut of spiritual, psychological and physical 'ailments' (O'Donnell, 1997:83). Thérèse was in so much physical and mental pain prior to her death from tuberculosis at 24 years of age that she even contemplated thoughts of suicide. Thérèse confided to her sister, Mother Agnes: "What would become of me if God did not give me courage? A person does not know what this is unless he [she] experiences it. No, it has to be experienced!" Jamart (1961:172) recounts Thérèse's acceptance of her 'lot', "The cross has followed me from the cradle ... but Jesus has taught me to love it passionately." Thérèse's own healing experiences enabled her to be sympathetic to the needs of her fellow sisters in religion. Spears (1998:4) maintains that healing in servant leadership is about wholeness.

Thérèse possessed the skill of healing, in relation to her own healing, and her desire to restore 'wholeness' to her novices, by catering to their personal, spiritual and psychological needs.

AWARENESS

Hildegard

Hildegard had experienced visions from early childhood but there was one visionary experience that changed her life forever. Hildegard experienced this spiritual awakening in 1141 some five years after her election as prioress in 1136. "When I was forty-two years and seven months old, heaven was opened and a fiery light of exceeding brilliance came and permeated my whole brain, and inflamed my whole heart and my whole breast, not like a burning but a warming flame, as the sun warms anything its rays touch" (cited in *Scivias*, 1990:59).

According to Degler (2007:5): "Hildegard's profound mystical experience in 1141 was significant not only because it brought with it a greater level of illumination, but also because the voice in the vision commanded her to 'say and write' what she 'saw and heard' in her visions." A leader who fosters awareness is cognizant of the existential reality and endeavours to promote wholeness and harmony [even] where there might be, uncertainty and lack of faith (Cameron, 2012).

Catherine

Catherine was sensitive to the reality within and the reality without (Noffke, 1980). Her incredible awareness was her innate knowledge of the spirituality of her times (Bynum, 1987). Raymond (cited in Kearns, 1980:29) recounts Catherine had her first recorded mystic experience, which occurred when she was about six years old. Noffke (1980:4) writes of Catherine's mystic espousal to Christ. Fink (2000b:106) describes the event: "Mary took her hand and held it up to Christ, who placed a ring on it making her his bride." Catherine's general awareness, including her self-knowledge, was so sensitive that Raymond (cited in Kearns, 1980:121) maintains that she often "fell into that state of body which is called ecstasy."

Catherine cultivated awareness, through her intuitive insight, through her knowledge of the spirituality of her times, and her mystical experiences, and through her general, self and spiritual awareness.

Teresa

Teresa's soul was awakened (Peers, 1963a:54). This spiritual awareness resulted in visionary experiences (Ahlgren, 1996:101). Teresa's awareness also extended to her interconnectedness with her nuns and her supporters and all she 'touched' during the existential reality of her time – and beyond (Spears, 1998:119). Teresa was the recipient of many favours, during which she experienced a sense of the presence of God. She experienced these favours when she was at prayer, either picturing an image of Christ, picturing praying with Him in the

Garden prior to His passion, or when reading. Teresa's interpretation of these events was that she was aware of a sense of God within her, and that she and the Divine presence were one: "This was in no sense a vision: I believe it is called mystical theology" (Peers, 1963a:58).

Teresa possessed the skill of awareness, which she developed through general and self-awareness and through sensitivity to the reality within and the reality without, resulting in a spiritual awakening which transported her to another reality – a mystical reality.

Thérèse

Thérèse experienced a spiritual awakening on the occasion of her conversion (DeMeester and Conroy, 1998:65): "This awareness gave Thérèse the insight that she 'had discovered once again the strength of soul which she had lost at the age of four and a half and [which] she was to preserve … forever'" (Clarke, 1996:98). DeGraaf et al. (2001:9) describe awareness as: "appreciating all that is going on around us and inside of us." O'Donnell (2001:20-21) observes: "one cannot but be struck by an aspect of Thérèse's personality that we in a wide sense call 'contemplative'. This emerges from an early age … but this natural reserve and her pleasure at being alone with her thoughts, in time opened up to genuine religious reflection and prayer."

Thérèse possessed the skill of awareness and cultivated it through her general awareness of the needs of her novices and through her own spiritual and self-awareness.

Persuasion

Hildegard

In her book *Jutta & Hildegard: The Biographical Sources*, Silvas (1998:xviii) includes information from the document referred to as the *Acta Inquisitionis* which "is the fruit of early efforts made towards Hildegard's canonization, that is the formal authentication and proclamation of her sanctity." The document lists a host of miracle reports which would have been forthcoming from witnesses called to give testimony during attempts to have Hildegard canonised (ibid.).

Hildegard's persuasion techniques are evidenced by testimonials from witnesses to her life and works; through her influence in persuading others to support her endeavours; through her charismatic personality and through her persuasive letter writing.

Catherine

The persuasive power of Catherine is exemplified by her charism and in her many letters, of which close to four hundred are still in existence (Noffke, 2000, 2001, 2007 & 2008). Catherine's influence extended to popes and kings and queens and many others who were the recipients of her letters. From the very beginning of her public ministry, Catherine was able to articulate her vision (Noffke, 2000:244-240) to reform the Church, to return the papacy to Rome and to raise support for a crusade – this was her mission. Catherine's followers were her 'spiritual family' who often referred to Catherine as 'mother' (Cameron, 2012:149).

Catherine possessed the skill of persuasion, evident in the testimonials of those who knew her, in her charism, and in her numerous letters.

Teresa

Persuasive tools in regard to the life of Teresa include the testimonials from the process of her canonisation which revealed the influence of her literary works on the "theological climate of the late sixteenth century" (Weber, 1990:5). In her writing Teresa used 'verbal camouflage' as a subterfuge to avoid being called before the Inquisition (Cameron, 2012:107). Teresa's persuasive tactics were also fully utilised in the establishment of her foundations (Peers, 1963c) and in her charismatic appeal (Ahlgren, 1996:8).

Teresa possessed the skill of persuasion, which is evidenced through testimonials from witnesses to her life, through her work, through her efforts to establish her foundations, and through her charismatic personality.

Thérèse

Forty-eight witnesses were interviewed for the 'Process of Beatification' for Thérèse of Lisieux (O'Mahony, 1975:7). The testimony of the witnesses is reflective of "the effectiveness of testimonials as a persuasion technique" (Hershey, 1993:10-14). Thérèse's persuasive tactics to enter Carmel by 'flaunting' protocol and actually speaking out to the then Holy Father, Leo XIII (Clarke, 1996:135), showed her determination to influence those in authority. Thérèse's charismatic appeal has influenced generations of followers. Thérèse's persuasive skills have been particularly apparent since her death. Mother Agnes (Pauline) emphasised to the members of the process for Thérèse's cause for beatification that numerous letters were received each day at Carmel and that thousands of copies of Thérèse's autobiography had been sold.

Thérèse's charismatic influence has been particularly evident through the many testimonials of witnesses at the process for her beatification and through the continuing devotion of generations of followers of her 'Little Way'.

CONCEPTUALISATION

Hildegard

Hildegard received formal recognition of her gifts and papal approval of her writing from Pope Eugenius III. Newman (1990:13) emphasises that "The importance of this papal seal of approval cannot be overestimated. Not only did it increase Hildegard's confidence and security in the face of continuing self-doubt, but it also authenticated her publicly and protected her from the censure she was bound to attract for violating the deuteron-Pauline stricture on female silence and submission." For St Paul states: "women should be silent in the churches. For they are not permitted to speak, but should be subordinate, as the law also says. If there is anything they desire to know, let them ask their husbands at home. For it is shameful for a woman to speak in church" [1 Cor., 14:34].

Hildegard's conceptualisation skills are evident through her mission, which was to reform the Church through being proactive and questioning – she was not content with the status quo. She challenged the 'prevailing order'. Hildegard thought beyond the day-to-day realities to realise her dreams for the future and her vision which was to have a united and reformed Church.

Catherine

Catherine's conceptualising skills resulted in her inspiriting others – (Greenleaf, cited in Frick and Spears, 1996:45), in her expressing voice through her letters (Noffke, 2000, 2001, 2007 and 2008); and in her looking at the big picture of reform for the Church – the return of the papacy to Rome and in her support of a crusade (Noffke, 1980). According to Noffke (2000:xiii) Catherine had a dream from early childhood which had centred on a life of quiet union with God. As a teenager she was accepted into the *Mantellate* a group of Dominican laywomen committed to the service of the poor and sick of the city. Catherine's biographer, Raymond (cited in Kearns, 1980:50), also recounted a dream of Catherine's when she was deciding on an order to enter. In the dream St Dominic approached her and with words of comfort, informed her that "you will one day wear this habit which you long for" (ibid.).

Catherine possessed the skill of conceptualisation through her mission to reform the Church, her efforts to have the papacy return to Rome and through her support of a crusade.

Teresa

The 'big picture' for Teresa was her vision for the Carmelite Order, the founding of her convents and her literary works (Fink, 2000b:119/123-124). Ahlgren (1996:35-36) maintains that it is not possible to know the exact time when Teresa decided to replace the mitigated rule with the primitive rule, although the idea had attracted her for many years. In his report written after Teresa's death, Father Domingo Báñez refers to the spirit that energised Teresa to be visionary and to be proactive. He quotes from an address she made to her nuns "I come solely to serve and please you in every possible way that I can ... I am a daughter of this house and a sister of you all. I know the character and the needs of you all, or, at least, of the majority of you (cited in Peers, 1963a:337).

Teresa possessed the skill of conceptualisation which is evidenced through her efforts to reform the Carmelite Order, and through the realisation of her plans to establish her foundations.

Thérèse

The 'big picture' for Thérèse was consolidated by her discovery of her 'Little Way' (O'Donnell, 1997:168) which became her legacy to future generations as did her autobiography which proclaimed her teaching to the world (Clarke, 1996). In her testimonial Mother Agnes (Thérèse's sister Pauline) states Thérèse's influence did not just extend to the members of the Carmel at Lisieux, but that her influence was 'felt' by people from all walks of life: "Some look on her as their guardian angel and have tangible proof of her continual assistance.

For these her writings are a code of perfection and they try to follow 'her way'" (cited in O'Mahony, 1975:70).

Thérèse possessed the skill of conceptualisation through the teaching of her "Little Way", and through her efforts to fulfil her mission to spend her heaven doing 'good' on earth.

FORESIGHT

Hildegard

Flanagan (1998:154-155) makes reference to Hildegard's 'monastic correspondents' and suggests there are some who "make explicit mention of Hildegard's prophetic gifts." Flanagan quotes from a letter to Hildegard by "Adam of Ebrach … expressing his concern about how to care for his monks, [and] refers in closing to 'the gift of the Holy Spirit, which works many marvels in you by the spirit of prophecy'" Flanagan (1998:155) suggests that Hildegard's prophetic gift enabled her to foresee the future and that "Although there are many difficulties in dating individual letters, her [Hildegard's] correspondence covers the years from around the Council of Trier [in 1148] to the end of her life" (p. 214).

Hildegard demonstrated foresight through her visionary leadership and her prophetic gifts. Pope Benedict (2010a:1-2) refers to Hildegard as a "'prophetess' who also speaks with great timeliness to us today, with her courageous ability to discern the signs of the times, her love for creation, her medicine, her poetry, her music … her love for Christ and for his Church which was suffering in that period too, wounded also in that time by the sins of both priests and lay people."

Catherine

Catherine possessed the charism of prophecy (Raymond, Kearns, 1980) and she seemed to have the ability to foresee an event before it happened. She could "sense the unknowable and foresee the unforeseeable" (Greenleaf, 2002:35). Catherine wrote a number of letters to Pope Gregory XI, requesting that he return the Papacy from Avignon to Rome. However she was unaware that "Gregory had already made up his mind, but he was one who placed great store by prophetic voices, and Catherine's insistence that he must return certainly strongly influenced the actual move" (Noffke, 1980:6).

Catherine possessed the skill of foresight, through her intuitive insight and her "charism of prophecy"; however her gift of "intuitive insight" was not always accurate (Raymond of Capua cited in Kearns, 1980). When Pope Gregory XI promulgated a Bull on 1 July 1375 calling for a crusade to save the Holy Land Catherine supported this crusade believing that it would be a reality but it did not eventuate. Raymond recalls that Catherine did not give a set time "for the coming to pass of any event which she ever foretold … [She] left that entirely to divine providence" and Raymond maintained that her critics had been too harsh (cited in Kearns, 1980:268-271).

Teresa

Teresa was a visionary. Ahlgren (1996:151) refers to Teresa's prophetic gifts and her 'foreknowledge of events' as testified by witnesses at the process for her canonisation. Teresa was intuitive to her own needs, and to those of her sisters in religion. Weber (1990:124-126) writes of Teresa's preoccupation with the past (the traditional system), the present (founding her convents in poverty), and the future (being chronicler of the reform). Spears (1998:5) describes foresight as the "characteristic that enables the servant-leader to understand the lessons from the past, the realities of the present, and the likely consequence of a decision for the future."

Teresa cultivated foresight through her sense of self and her prophetic gifts, and through her relationship with others in sharing her vision.

Thérèse

Thérèse had visionary experiences (Clarke, 1996) at various stages throughout her life, which included: an 'event' which involved her father when she was a child, a 'miracle' performed by the Mother of God, her Act of Oblation to Merciful Love and her ecstatic experience on her deathbed.

Thérèse's intuitive insight told her that she would return to the world (after her death). "I will return! I will come down … 'I feel my mission is about to begin, my mission of making others love God as I love him, my mission of teaching my little way to souls … I want to spend my heaven in doing good on earth'" (Clarke, 1996:263).

Thérèse felt within her many vocations but there was a special vocation she spoke about to her sister Cèline known as Sister Geneviève of Saint Teresa:

> In 1897, but before she was really ill, Sister Thérèse told me she expected to die that year … When she realized that she had pulmonary tuberculosis, she said: "You see, God is going to take me at an age when I would not have had the time to become a priest … If I could have been a priest, I would have been ordained at these June ordinations. So, what did God do? So that I would not be disappointed, he let me be sick: in that way I couldn't have been there, and I would die before I could exercise my ministry." The sacrifice of not being able to be a priest was something she always felt deeply … "Oh! What wonders we shall see in heaven! I have a feeling that those who desired to be priests on earth will be able to share in the honour of the priesthood in heaven" (cited in O'Mahony, 1975:155-156).

Thérèse possessed the skill of foresight through prophetic awareness, through her intuition and through sharing and serving vision.

Stewardship

Hildegard

Hildegard's works – her eminent doctrine – have been held in trust over many generations. This stewardship of her resources by members of the Benedictine Order has enabled Hildegard's message to be read and heard across the centuries. For as a *Doctor of the Universal Church* her teaching is relevant not just for her own times but for all time.

Hildegard took her leadership responsibilities seriously for she did not just serve her sisters in religion and the public. She served creation. Sims (1997:145) wisely advocates that stewardship should encompass more than just the 'trappings' of leadership, and that servant leaders should endeavour to serve creation: "[We should] seize our vocation of stewardship of the earth as a divine calling, that we learn to care for creation as servant leaders."

Hildegard was steward of the "human and institutional resources entrusted to her care" (Stubbs, cited in Spears, 1998:316) and she demonstrated this stewardship through her quest to reform the Church and the clergy, through the legacy of her writings and through her two foundations.

Catherine

Catherine left her work and in particular her 'book', *The Dialogue* in trust for future generations. Her mission was one of service and stewardship (Noffke, 1980). In *The Dialogue*, God appoints Catherine as the steward of his people (Noffke, 1980:159), and Catherine responds by doing everything in her power to serve the people entrusted to her care. Catherine revealed God's truth, as spoken to her in *The Dialogue*, to all who would listen to the words which she dictated to her scribes. Her ministry revolved around service, and she performed this service in relation to God, Church, neighbour, self and created things (Noffke, 2000, 2001, 2007 & 2008).

Catherine was custodian of God's truth, and she was constantly in touch with God during the times she ministered to the poor and needy, when she offered advice to people at every level of social standing, and when she valiantly persevered in her determination to fulfil the wishes of "Christ on earth" (the Pope).

Catherine cultivated stewardship through her efforts as an agent of change and in her quest for reform of the Church and its clergy.

Teresa

During her lifetime Teresa was steward of the people in her care, particularly her nuns to whom she entrusted her legacy of prayer (Peers, 1963b). Teresa set in trust a responsible stewardship (Greenleaf, 1977:241) by her efforts to achieve her goals in spite of continued opposition and resistance from ecclesial and civic authorities (Ahlgren, 1996). Teresa was a steward and custodian of the past richness of her order, because she ensured, by her reform, that the legacy of the past would be maintained into the future. Ahlgren (1996:165) refers to Teresa's contribution to the institutional Church which, she maintains, found in Teresa "a powerful spokesperson for the counter-Reformation Church."

Teresa cultivated stewardship, through her legacy to her nuns and the Church, and by being an agent of change in the establishment of her seventeen foundations.

Thérèse

Therese's way of life; her autobiography; her teaching – *Story of a Soul* (Clarke, 1996) and her impact on generations of followers of her 'Little Way' have established her stewardship in the service of the Church. O'Donnell (1997:212) states that "'The Little Way' and her 'Offering to Merciful Love' have entered into the mainstream of Catholic spirituality.'" Spears (1998:xiv) writes about redefining "leadership as service and stewardship." Thérèse was a steward of Scripture. Her "Little Way of Spiritual Childhood" had its inception in Scripture, which she discovered when reading Old Testament texts in a notebook belonging to Céline her sister (Jamart,1961:32). Thérèse's stewardship has influenced the spirituality in the Church in the century following her death, and continues to be influential in her role as patroness of the missions. She is also one of the patrons of World Youth Day which is an international Catholic event for young people celebrated every three years.

Thérèse cultivated stewardship through sharing vision and through her acceptance of the responsibility of being a steward of spiritual resources and of the novices in her care.

COMMITMENT TO THE GROWTH OF PEOPLE

Hildegard

In his Apostolic Letter Proclaiming St Hildegard of Bingen a *Doctor of the Universal Church* Pope Benedict XVI refers to Hildegard's spirituality "At the basis of her spirituality was the Benedictine Rule which views spiritual balance and ascetical moderation as paths to holiness" (2012a:1). Newman writes that when Hildegard was placed in Jutta's care as a child "She learned to read the Latin Bible, particularly the psalms, and to chant the monastic Office" (1990:11). Hildegard tells us that she received a limited education because she was taught by an *unlearned woman – Jutta* (Flanagan, 1995) and it was not until the visionary experience of her *Spiritual Awakening* that she received "infused knowledge of all the books of Scripture" (Newman, 1990:12).

Hildegard demonstrated her commitment to the growth of people, through developing the spiritual growth of herself and her sisters in religion, through her understanding of the needs of others, by nurturing and empowering those in her care and by giving witness to the mandate given to her by the living Light "Speak therefore of these wonders, and, being so taught, write them and speak" (*Scivias*, 1990:59).

Catherine

Mentoring and nurturing were aspects of Catherine's leadership in relationship to her team, her disciples. They in turn loved and respected her – Raymond (Kearns, 1980) and called her 'mother' (Noffke, 1980). Catherine was committed to their growth and believed that "Those served grow as persons ..." (Greenleaf, 1977:13). Catherine demonstrated her commitment to the growth of people when she assumed the responsibility for mentoring and nurturing, the spiritual, personal and professional growth of those close to her, particularly her disciples. Cavallini (1998:10) stresses that Catherine understood the needs of others, and knew "how and when to praise or to blame or to soothe."

Catherine cultivated commitment to the growth of people, through her understanding of the needs of others, through her mentoring and fostering the talents of others, and through her nurturing and empowering those in her care.

Teresa

Teresa was committed to the growth of her nuns, and in particular, their spiritual growth. She engaged a network of supporters in her efforts at reform (Ahlgren, 1996:2). Teresa did not just lead as an individual; she led as part of a collective group (Fairholm and Fairholm, 2000:102). Teresa was committed to the spiritual progress and growth of her nuns, and wrote a book, the *Way of Perfection*, for the members of her community to guide them in their life of prayer and thus provide them with some spiritual direction (Peers,1963b). The testimonials given to promote Teresa's Cause for canonisation stated (Peers, 1963c) that Teresa did not just delegate tasks but did her own share – whether it was sweeping floors or cooking meals, or doing various other menial tasks, even when her health was poor. In this way, Teresa was teaching her nuns the value of service to others. This form of service in leadership reflects servant leadership.

Teresa cultivated commitment to the growth of people through her commitment to her own spiritual growth and that of her nuns, and through developing the skills and potential of her nuns, through mentoring and nurturing.

Thérèse

Thérèse was committed to the growth of the people she guided; in particular her novices. Thérèse in a conversation with Mother Agnes (O'Mahony, 1975:31-32) states: "I scatter the good seed that God gives me among my little birds, and then let events take their course without worrying any more about the outcome." Greenleaf (Fraker and Spears, 1996:37) emphasises that "Both leader and follower respect the integrity and allow the autonomy of the other."

In her leadership role, Thérèse was responsible for the novices who were from various walks of life and who included her sister Céline and cousin, Marie Guérin (Clarke,1996). Though Thérèse was not officially the novice mistress, she was given the responsibility of acting novice mistress, but for all intents and purposes she was in charge of the novices. Thérèse fulfilled her duties to the best of her ability.

Thérèse cultivated commitment to the growth of people through the mentoring and nurturing of her novices, through her commitment to the spiritual growth of others, and through the promotion of her "Little Way".

Building Community

Hildegard

During the Homily at the Holy Mass for the opening of the Synod of Bishops and Proclamation of St John of Ávila and St Hildegard of Bingen as 'Doctors of the Church' Pope Benedict reinforces the words of Pope St John Paul II in 1979 when he described St Hildegard as a "Light for her people and her time" and not just for her time but as a role model for women and men in the contemporary Church: "Saint Hildegard of Bingen, an important female figure of the twelfth century, offered her precious contribution to the growth of the Church of her time, employing the gifts received from God and showing herself to be a woman of brilliant intelligence deep sensitivity and recognised spiritual authority" (2012:2).

Hildegard demonstrated building community through living in a community and following the Benedictine Rule, through building up the community of the Church by her efforts at reform, through her apostolic, pastoral activity, and through establishing two monasteries during her lifetime. Hildegard's proclamation as a Doctor of the Church has contributed significantly to the building of the Church community.

Catherine

Catherine demonstrated building community by nurturing her disciples, and by taking the Church out to the people. Words from *The Dialogue* state, "Each of you must work for the salvation of souls according to your own situation" (Noffke, 1980:127). Catherine's writings, her teachings, her spirituality, her love of God, love of neighbour, and love of Church, all were instrumental in assisting her mission, as mediator and 'pacifist', for the Church, thereby assisting in its growth by building community.

Unlike Hildegard who founded two convents and Teresa, who founded seventeen convents, Catherine established just one convent. Catherine lived her life for the Church. Her love for God, Church and the universe, have been well-documented over the years, by scholars who have studied and researched her work and through the mediation of her disciples. Catherine was a leader builder who took the time to build her community, her team (Noffke, 2000, 2001, 2007 & 2008). Catherine made a difference and in the words of Blanchard and Hodges (2003:11) by her "personal response to Jesus' call to 'Follow Me' … [Catherine] put into action the principles of Servant Leadership."

Catherine cultivated building community, through her apostolic activity, and through her efforts at renewal, and rebuilding the Dominican community. Catherine's proclamation as a Doctor of the Church has contributed significantly to the building of the Church community.

Teresa

Teresa contributed to the building community of the Church by her commitment to the Church. Teresa's sense of Church was evident in the seventeen convents she founded. Keith Egan (1998:147-148) comments "her monasteries … served as local churches for her daughters." Egan describes these monasteries as "little churches … [They] were a vision of what Teresa meant by being church." And again: "Teresa pictured her monasteries as 'Little Dovecotes' where God sends abundant mystical gifts" (Egan, 1998:157). Teresa was a builder of communities as is evidenced by her many foundations which were established at great personal, physical and emotional cost (Peers, 1963c). Teresa was also a builder of people as is evidenced by her efforts to "challenge the status quo" (Ahlgren, 1996).

For Teresa, a new convent was a house of God. Teresa founded a number of these 'houses' and set her seal on the future of the discalced Carmelites, who in the contemporary Church have convents scattered throughout the world. Teresa cultivated building community through building up her community of nuns and through her visionary endeavours. Teresa's proclamation as a Doctor of the Church has contributed significantly to the building of the Church community.

Thérèse

To build community it is necessary to first of all build people (Taulbert, 2008:36). Thérèse worked with the members of her community to 'serve her vision' (Blanchard and Hodges, 2003:68). DeMeester (2002:9) explains that "towards the end of her life she developed a highly generous, all-encompassing apostolic awareness with a primary emphasis on the neighbors whom she saw every day – her community." Thérèse demonstrated building community by her efforts to maintain peace and harmony within her religious community, and by teaching her novices a sense of community. Unlike Hildegard, Teresa and Catherine, Thérèse did not found any convents, but spent virtually her whole life in a single convent. Thérèse was born into a religious household that was "run rather like a convent" (Monica Furlong, 1987:5). The family lived for the Church, and for religion. Both Thérèse's parents Louis and Zélie were beatified in 2008 and in June 2015 Pope Francis approved "the decrees for the canonization of Louis and Zelie Martin" (Vatican Radio, 2015).

Thérèse cultivated building community through her living in community and through her teaching her novices to work as a team. Thérèse made holiness accessible to all. Thérèse's proclamation as a Doctor of the Church has contributed significantly to the building of the Church community.

There are similarities and differences when the ten core

characteristics of servant leadership are applied to the lives and works of Hildegard of Bingen, Catherine of Siena, Teresa of Ávila, and Thérèse of Lisieux. However all four women were leaders within their communities and the *Snapshot Comparison* shows that their leadership practices reflect the ten core characteristics of the servant leadership paradigm.

17

Conclusion

St Hildegard of Bingen

Though Hildegard was a loyal and committed member of an institution (the Church) whose governing body was and is based on hierarchical principles, she was able to practise servant leadership within her own milieu. The servant leadership approach to leadership has been most effective in that its focus on the leader as servant fulfils the mandate of Christ (Matthew, 20:26-28): "whoever wishes to be first among you must be your slave; just as the Son of Man came not to be served but to serve, and to give his life a ransom for many." In other words leadership is an act of service (Blanchard and Hodges, 2003:12).

In her critique of Greenleaf's concept of servant leadership Yvonne Bradley (1999:44) comments on Greenleaf being influenced, "by religious understandings of leadership which he contends are just as relevant in the secular realm as they purport to be in the sacred: 'Greenleaf's philosophy is unabashedly spiritual, yet it's finding a home in the secular world of the corporation' (Lee and Zemke, 1993:22). These leadership ideals are replicated in the teachings of numerous religions and philosophies – including Islam, Zen and Taoism – and in the thoughts and understandings of leaders like Mahatma Gandhi" who contend that religion and spirituality can influence the leadership practices within faith-based and secular organisations.

Bradley (1999:47) maintains that because the servant leadership concept tends to be used broadly, therein lay the flaws, "It could also be argued that Greenleaf's original writings are not necessarily in fundamental opposition to hierarchical organisational structures. True, leaders are servants and their 'right' to lead is granted by the followers in response to their leaders' servant disposition. Nevertheless, the concept of hierarchy, of lines of authority and responsibility, is not a significant issue for Greenleaf" and obviously it was not an issue for Hildegard (see above).

Bradley (1999:52; cited in Cameron, 2009) suggests that a leader who displays the characteristics of servant leadership might be seen as:

> weak and indecisive ... Undue emphasis on the servant aspect of leadership, whether in the mirage of Greenleaf's ill-defined concept or in the more precisely drawn biblical interpretation, runs the risk of blinding educationists to the many responsibilities and predicaments of their leadership. Leadership sometimes demands bold action, harsh decisions, courage, risks, ignoring the opinion of others ... It sometimes involves deep regrets, difficult negotiations and disappointing compromises.

Undoubtedly after applying the ten core characteristics to her life and works it is evident that Hildegard could be described as bold and outspoken. She had courage and she took risks. She negotiated, compromised and on occasion ignored the opinion of others. However in her writings she does not come across as weak or indecisive in fact the opposite is true. So then where does Hildegard stand in relation to the concept of servant leadership?

Sims (1997:16) describes Jesus Christ as "the prototype of the servant leader" and one just has to read scripture to see the qualities and values that defined the leadership of Jesus. Indeed according to Blanchard and Hodges (2003:51): "Jesus lived His values of love of God and love of His neighbor all the way to the cross ... No greater love has any man then to lay down His life for His friends (John

15:13).'" The leadership of Jesus Christ then was not 'weak and/or indecisive'. And leaders would do well to emulate His love, faith, strength and courage in their service to those they lead. So given the basis then of Christian service demonstrated in the exemplary servanthood of Christ the approach to servant leadership which Greenleaf conceptualised almost forty years ago is surely an ideal form of leadership for the Christian leader, with its emphasis on service (cited in Cameron, 2012:9).

The Catholic Church has canonised thousands of saints (Cameron, 2012:5) and proclaimed just thirty-six doctors. So why was Hildegard of Bingen, chosen for the honour of being selected to join this 'elite' group within the Church? Well you may recall from Chapter 4 that Hildegard fulfilled the required criteria and so has the confidence of the Church. In addition during her lifetime and as a member of the Benedictine Order Hildegard produced an incredible volume of work and possessed many gifts and talents that she used in sharing and serving vision to the clergy, her sisters in religion and to the general community. Her nationality was German and at the time of the consideration of her proclamation as a Doctor of the Church the Pope, Benedict XVI was German also and from what we have seen in this book Pope Benedict greatly admired this Saint of Bingen and her works. Also Hildegard had been referred to as a saint from very early times and by approving the 'equivalent canonisation' in May 2012, Benedict was just formalising a process that had begun centuries before.

Though it could be said that Hildegard exhibited all the characteristics of servant leadership and really what we have read also suggests orthodoxy in her work and some conservatism regarding the Church – she was and still is an enigma – and during her lifetime was subject to 'extremes of behaviour'. Perhaps the years in the 'anchorhold' combined with the times in which she lived had an impact and added to the development of a multi-faceted personality which comes across as forceful but also at times self-doubting and questioning. Nevertheless Hildegard had inner strength and not content with the status quo was prepared to step outside her comfort zone to deliver the message of the Living Light (*Scivias*, 1990).

Greenleaf (cited in Fraker and Spears, 1996:4) maintains that "inspired, prophetic institutional leadership begins with one spirit-filled faithful person, who will be strong enough to strike out on a different path, leading the institution down that path" (cited in Cameron, 2012:36). Servant leadership incorporates the best aspects of many models of leadership including spiritual leadership, charismatic leadership and transformational leadership. The emphasis on leadership in the twenty-first century is increasingly on people relationships and on building community (Taulbert, 2008:40) – sentiments reflected in servant leadership. The challenge for leaders today is to be open to change. However as argued by Edgar Schein (1999:168) change cannot happen overnight. Leaders might do well to remember that "The journey of a thousand miles begins with a single step" (Tao Te Ching, cited in Heider, 1985:xi).

Hildegard of Bingen died on 17 September 1179 at the convent at Rupertsberg. Silvas writes that in the "account of Hildegard's death … the style is generally simple and unadorned [and] short on concrete information" (1998:124). Quoting from the book of Hildegard's life (*Vita*) Silvas recounts the sentiments of her sisters in religion at Hildegard's passing to eternal life:

> When the blessed mother had devotedly waged battle for the Lord with many difficult struggles, she felt the weariness of this present life and daily *yearned to be dissolved and to be with Christ* … God graciously heeded her longing, and as it had been her wish, by the spirit of prophecy revealed to her end, which she foretold to her sisters.

She had laboured in illness for some time, when in the eighty-second year of her life, on the … [17 September], she departed with a happy passage to her heavenly spouse. Her daughters, to whom she had been all joy and solace, wept bitterly as they took part in the funeral rites of their beloved mother (1998:209).

The message of Hildegard to contemporary leaders is clear – 'let the light within you shine' so that your ministry of leadership will always be illumined by the '*Voice* of the *Living Light*'!

GLOSSARY

DOCTORS OF THE UNIVERSAL CHURCH (SEPTEMBER 2015)

(The Doctors are listed in the order of the year of their births and not the year of their Proclamations)

1.	St Athanasius (c.297-373)	19.	St Peter Damian (c.1007-1072)
2.	St Ephrem (c.306-c.373)	20.	St Anselm (1033-1109)
3.	St Cyril of Jerusalem (c.315-386)	21.	St Bernard of Clairvaux (c.1090-1153)
4.	St Hilary of Poitiers (c.315-c.368)	22.	*St Hildegard of Bingen* (c.1098-1179)
			* Proclaimed 7 October 2012
5.	St Gregory of Nazianzen (c.329-c.389)	23.	St Anthony of Padua (1195-1231)
6.	St Basil the Great (c.329-379)	24.	St Albert the Great (c.1206-1280)
7.	St Ambrose (c.340-397)	25.	St Bonaventure (c.1221-1274)
8.	St Jerome (c.342-c.420)	26.	St Thomas Aquinas (c.1225-1274)
9.	St John Chrysostom (c.347-407)	27.	*St Catherine of Siena* (1347-1380)
			* Proclaimed 4 October 1970
10.	St Augustine (354-430)	28.	St John of Ávila (1499-1569)
11.	St Cyril of Alexandria (c.376-444)	29.	*St Teresa of Ávila* (1515-1582)
			* Proclaimed 27 September 1970
12.	Pope St Leo the Great (c.400-461)	30.	St Peter Canisius (1521-1597)
13.	St Peter Chrysologus (c.406-c.450)	31.	St Robert Bellarmine (1542-1621)
14.	Pope St Gregory the Great (c.540-604)	32.	St John of the Cross (1542-1591)

15.	St Isidore of Seville (c.560-636)	33.	St Lawrence of Brindisi (1559-1619)
16.	St Bede the Venerable (c.673-735)	34.	St Francis de Sales (1567-1622)
17.	St John Damascene (c.676-c.749)	35.	St Alphonsus Liguori (1696-1787)
18.	St Gregory of Narek (c.951-1003)	36.	*St Thérèse of Lisieux* (1873-1897)
			* Proclaimed 19 October 1997

With the exception of St John of Ávila, St Hildegard of Bingen and St Gregory of Narek (the three most recent candidates admitted to the doctoral ranks) the above list is taken from:

Rengers, C. 2000, *The 33 Doctors of the Church*, Tan Books and Publishers, Inc. Illinois, USA.

REFERENCES

Abbott, G., 2014, "Hildegard of Bingen", *ABC Classic FM: Keys to Music*, September 28. Retrieved 15 January 2015 from http://www.abc.net.au/classic/content/2014/09/28/4047546.htm

Abbott, W. (ed), 1967, *The Documents of Vatican II*, Chapman, London.

Ahlgren, G.T., 1996, *Teresa of Avila and the Politics of Sanctity*, Cornell University Press, U.S.A.

Antonakis, J., Cianciolo, A., Sternberg, R. (eds), 2004, *The Nature of Leadership*, Sage Publications, Inc., California.

Anzalone, F.M., 2007, "Servant Leadership: A New Model for Law Library Leaders", *Law Library*, vol. 99, no. 48, pp. 793-812. Retrieved 29 July 2008 from Heinonline database.

Baird, J.L., 2006, *The Personal Correspondence of Hildegard of Bingen*, Oxford University Press Inc., U.S.A.

Bass, B.M., 1981, *Stogdill's handbook of leadership*, (Revised Edition), The Free Press, New York.

Batten, J., 1998, "Servant-Leadership: A Passion to Serve", in *Insights on Leadership: Service, Stewardship, Spirit, and Servant-Leadership*, (ed) L. C. Spears, John Wiley & Sons, Inc., U.S.A., pp. 38-53.

Beare, H., 2006, "Leadership for a New Millennium", *ACEL Monograph Leading and Managing*, no. 38, pp. 1-22.

Benedict XVI, 2010a, "Saint Hildegard of Bingen", *General Audience*. Papal Summer Residence, Castel Gandolfo, September 1. Retrieved 8 March 2013 from http://www.hildegard.org/BenedictXVI/BenedictXVI.html

Benedict XVI, 2010b, "Saint Hildegard of Bingen (2)", *General Audience*. Paul VI Hall, September 8. Retrieved 8 March 2013 from http://www.hildegard.org/BenedictXVI/BenedictXVI.html

Benedict XVI, 2010c, "Sala Regia", *Address of His Holiness Benedict XVI on the occasion of Christmas Greetings to the Roman Curia* December 20.

Benedict XVI, 2012a, "Proclaiming Saint Hildegard of Bingen, professed nun of the Order of Saint Benedict, a Doctor of the Universal Church", *Apostolic Letter*, October 7. Retrieved 9 January 2013 from http://w2.vatican.

va/content/benedict-xvi/en/apost_letters/documents/hf_ben-xvi_ apl_20121007_ildegarda-bingen.html

Benedict XVI, 2012b, "The Opening of the Synod of Bishops and Proclamation of St John of Avila and of St Hildegard of Bingen as 'Doctors of the Church", *Holy Mass*, October 7. Retrieved 9 January 2013 from http://www.news.va/en/news/holy-mass-for-the-opening-of-the-synod-of-bishops

Bennis, W., 1959, "leadership theory and administrative behavior", in *Administrative Science Quarterly*, vol. 4, no. 3, pp. 259-301.

Bennis, W. & Nanus, B., 1985, *Leaders: The strategies for change*, Harper and Row, New York.

Betti, U., 1981, "Preserve the True Meaning of the Canonical Requisites", *L'Osservatore Romano*, English Language Edition, 29 June, no. 3.

Blanchard, K., 2007, *Leading at a Higher Level*, Prentice Hall, New Jersey.

Blanchard, K. & Hodges, P., 2003, *The Servant Leader: Transforming Your Heart, Head, Hands & Habits*, Countryman, Tennessee U.S.A.

Block, P., 1993, *Stewardship: Choosing service over self interest*. CA: Berrett-Koehler Publishing, San Francisco.

Bodie, G., 2011, "The Active-Empathetic Listening Scale (AELS): Conceptualization and Evidence of Validity Within the Interpersonal Domain", *Communication Quarterly*, vol. 59, no. 1-2, p. 279. Retrieved 4 February 2015 from http://www.tandfonline.com.ezproxy1.acu.edu.au/doi/pdf/10.1080/01463373.2011.583495

Boyd, J., 2012, *An Ecology of Educational Leadership*, February 2. Retrieved 19 February 2015 from http://julieboyd.com.au/an-ecology-of-educational-leadership

Bradley, Y., 1999, "Servant Leadership: A Critique of Robert Greenleaf's Concept of Leadership", *Journal of Christian Education*, vol. 42, no. 2 (September), pp. 42-54.

Brennan, W., (Trans), 2003, *Women Mystics of the Medieval Era An anthology*, St Paul's Publications, Australia.

Brooks, B., 2006, "The Power of Active Listening", *The American Salesman*, vol. 51, iss. 6, June, pp. 12-14. Retrieved 20 August 2008 from ProQuest database.

Burns, J.M., 1978, *Leadership*, Harper & Row, New York.

Butcher, C., 2013, *A Spiritual Reader St Hildegard of Bingen Doctor of the Church*, Paraclete Press, Brewster, Massachusetts, U.S.A.

Bynum, C.W., 1987, *Holy Feast and Holy Fast: The Religious Significance of Food to Medieval Women*, University of California Press, U.S.A.

Bynum, C.W., 1990, "Preface", in *Hildegard of Bingen: Scivias*, Hart, C. & Bishop, J. (Trans.), Paulist Press, U.S.A.

Cameron, C., 2009, "Women Doctors of the Catholic Church: A Study in Servant Leadership", *PhD Thesis*, CD-ROM, University of New England, Armidale, Australia.

Cameron, C., 2012, *Leadership as a call to service. The lives and works of Teresa of Ávila, Catherine of Siena and Thérèse of Lisieux*, Connor Court Publishing, Ballarat, Victoria.

Cameron, C., 2014, "Stewardship as Service", *Mission and Spirituality eNewsletter*, Broken Bay Institute, March 3, Edition 20. Retrieved from: http://www.bbi.catholic.edu.au/e-news/bbi-mission-and-spirituality-e-news/133-2014-02-28.html

Cameron, C., 2014, "Leadership as Service", *Catholic Viewpoint*, vol. 23, no. 1, autumn, Diocese of Armidale.

Capra, F., 1996, *The Web of Life*, p. 295, Doubleday, New York.

Catechism of the Catholic Church, 2000, *Pocket Edition* 2nd edn. St Pauls Publications NSW.

Catholic Bible Press, 1990, *Holy Bible: The New Revised Standard Version*, Thomas Nelson, Inc., U.S.A.

Cavallini, G., 1998, *Catherine of Siena*, Chapman, London.

Chopra, D., 2002, "The soul of leadership", *School Administrator*, vol. 59, iss. 8, p. 10. Retrieved 17 August from ProQuest database.

Clarke, J., 1996, *Story of a Soul: The Autobiography of St Therese of Lisieux*, ICS Publications, Washington.

Conger, J.A. & Kanungo, R.N. & Menon, S.T., 2000, "Charismatic Leadership and Follower Effects", *Organizational Behavior*, vol. 21, no. 7, Nov., pp. 747-767. Retrieved 13 September 2008 from JSTOR database.

Congregation for the Clergy, 1997, *General Directory for Catechesis*, St. Paul's, NSW.

Covey, S., 1990, *The Seven Habits of Highly Effective People*. Provo, UT: Covey Leadership Center.

Covey, S., 2004, *The Seven Habits of Highly Effective People*, Simon & Schuster, New York.

Cunningham, L.S., 2005, *A Brief History of Saints*, Blackwell Publishing, U.S.A.

Daneault, S. 2008, "The wounded healer: Can this idea be of use to family physicians?" *Canadian Family Physician*, vol. 54, pp. 1218-1219. Retrieved 20 March 2009 from ProQuest database.

De Chardin, P. T., 1960, *The Divine Milieu*, p. 138, Harper & Brothers, New York.

De Chardin, P. T., 2004, in Stephen R. Covey, *The Seven Habits of Highly Effective People*, p. 319, Simon & Schuster, New York.

Degler, T., 2007, "Kundalini Awareness: St. Hildegard of Bingen", *Institute for Consciousness Research*. Retrieved 6 July 2014 from http://www.readbag.com/icrcanada-documents-sthilbingen

DeGraaf, D. & Tilley, C. & Neal, L., 2001, "Servant Leadership Characteristics in Organizational Life", The Greenleaf Center, Indiana, U.S.A.

DeMeester, C. & Conroy, S., 1998, *The Power of Confidence: Genesis and structure of the 'Way of Spiritual Childhood' of Saint Therese of Lisieux*, Alba House, New York.

DeMeester, C., 2002, *With Empty Hands: The Message of St Therese of Lisieux*, Burns & Oates, London.

Dronke, P., 1984, *Women Writers*, pp. 175-176, Cambridge University Press, New York.

Drucker, P.F., 2001, *Management Challenges for the Twenty-First Century*, Harper Business, New York.

Egan, K.J., 1998, "The ecclesiology of Teresa of Avila: Women as church especially in the book of her foundations", in *Theology: Expanding the Borders*, (eds) M. Aquino & R. Goizueta, "The Annual Publication of the College Theology Society", vol. 43, pp. 145-161.

Engen, J.V., 1998, in *Voice of the Living Light, Hildegard of Bingen and Her World*, (ed) B. Newman, University of California Press, California, U.S.A.

Fairholm M.R. & Fairholm, G., 2000, "Leadership amid the constraints of trust", *Leadership & Organization Development*, vol. 21, no. 2, pp. 102-109. Retrieved 2008 from Emerald database.

Fierro, N., 1997, *Hildegard of Bingen: Symphony of the Harmony of Heaven*. Retrieved 23 January 2014 from http://hildegard.org/music/music.html

Fink, J.F., 2000a, *The Doctors of The Church: Doctors of the First Millennium*, vol. 1, Alba House, New York.

Fink, J.F., 2000b, *The Doctors of the Church: Doctors of the Second Millennium*, vol. 2, Alba House, New York.

Flanagan, S., 1995, "Hildegard von Bingen (1098-1179)", In *German Writers and words of the Early Middle Ages*: 800-1170, vol. 148. University of Adelaide. Retrieved 23 January 2014 from http://hildegard.org/documents/flanagan.html

Flanagan, S., 1998, *Hildegard of Bingen (1098-1179): A Visionary* Life, January, 2nd edn. Routledge, New York.

Fordham University, *The Life and Works of Hildegard von Bingen (1098-1179)*. Retrieved 16 July 2014, from Internet History Sourcebooks Project. http://www.fordham.edu/halsall/med/hildegarde.asp

Fraker, A.T. & Spears, L.C., (eds), 1996, *Robert K. Greenleaf: Seeker and Servant: Reflections on Religious Leadership*, Jossey-Bass Publishers, San Francisco.

Frankl, V., 1959, *Man's search for meaning*, Simon and Schuster, New York.

Francis, 2015, "Proclaiming Saint Gregory of Narek, a Doctor of the Universal Church", *Apostolic Letter*, April 12. Retrieved 29 May 2015 from http://w2.vatican.va/content/francesco/la/apost_letters/documents/papa-francesco_lettera-ap_2015412_gregorius-narecensis-doctor-ecclesiae.html

Francis, 2015, Encyclical letter *Laudato Si' on care for our common home*. Retrieved 16 July 2015 from http://w2.vatican.va/content/francesco/en/encyclicals/documents/papa-francesco_20150524_enciclica-laudato-si.html

Frick, D.M. & Spears, L.C., (eds), 1996, *Robert K. Greenleaf: On Becoming A Servant-Leader*, Josey-Bass Publishers, San Francisco.

Furlong, M. 1987, *Therese of Lisieux*, Virago Press Limited, London.

Gardiner, J., 1998, "Quiet Presence: The Holy Ground of Leadership", in *Insights on Leadership: Service, Stewardship, Spirit, and Servant-Leadership*, (ed), L. C. Spears, John Wiley & Sons, Inc., U.S.A., pp. 116-125.

Greenleaf, R., 1977, *Servant Leadership: A Journey into the Nature of Legitimate Power and Greatness*, Paulist Press, New York.

Greenleaf, R., 1991, *Servant Leadership: A Journey into the Nature of Legitimate Power and Greatness*, Paulist Press, New York.

Greenleaf, R., 1998, "Servant-Leadership", in *Insights on Leadership: Service, Stewardship, Spirit, and Servant-Leadership,* (ed), L. C. Spears, John Wiley & Sons, Inc., U.S.A., pp. 15-20.

Greenleaf, R., 2002, *Servant Leadership: A Journey into the Nature of Legitimate Power and Greatness*, 25th edn, Paulist Press, New York.

Gronau, E., 1996, *Hildegard. Vita di una donna profetica alle origini dell'eta moderna,* Milan, p. 402.

Hackman, M. & Johnson, C., 2009, *Leadership: A Communication Perspective*, 5th edn, Waveland Press, Inc., Illinois.

Hamilton, J.W., 2006, "The Critical Effect of Object Loss in the Development of Episodic Manic Illness", *American Academy of Psychoanalysis and Dynamic Psychiatry*, vol. 34, no. 2, summer, p. 333. Retrieved 2008 from ProQuest database.

Hart, C. & Bishop, J, (Trans.), 1990, *Hildegard of Bingen: Scivias*, Paulist Press, U.S.A.

Harvey, M. & Riggio, R., 2011, *Leadership studies: The dialogue of a discipline.* Edward Elgar, Northampton, MA.

Hayton, M.S.J., 2015, "Inflections of Prophetic Vision: The Reshaping of Hildegard of Bingen's Apocalypticism as Represented by Abridgments of the *Pentachronon", Centre for Medieval Studies*, University of Toronto. Retrieved 13 May 2015 from http://www.academia.edu/10763619/Dissertation_Abstract_Hayton

Heider, J., 1985, *The Tao of Leadership. Lao Tzu's Tao Te Ching: Adapted for a New Age,* Humanics Ltd., U.S.A.

Hershey, R., 1993, "A practitioner's view of motivation", *Managerial Psychology*, vol. 8, iss. 3, pp. 10-14. Retrieved 10 September 2008, from ProQuest database.

Hesse, H., 1956, *The Journey to the East*, Peter Owen, London.

Hildegard, (n.d.), *A Prayer of Awareness.* Retrieved 16 July 2014 from http://www.webofcreation.org/Worship/liturgy/prayers.htm

Hodges, P., 2003, *The Servant Leader: Transforming Your Heart, Head, Hands & Habits*, Countryman, Tennessee U.S.A.

Hoyle, J.R. 2007, *Leadership and Futuring: Making Visions Happen*, 2nd edn, Corwin Press, California.

Huizenga, L., 2012, *St Hildegard of Bingen, Doctor of the Church*, October 4. Retrieved on 17 January, 2014 from Http://www.firstthings.com/onthesquare/2012/10/st-hildegard-of-hingen-doctor-of-the-church.

Hunt, M., 1998, *Dream Makers: Putting Vision and Values to work*, Davies Black Publisher, Palo Alto, CA.

Hunter, J.C., 2004, *The World's Most Powerful Leadership Principle: How to Become a Servant Leader*, Crown Business, New York.

Jamart, F. (Trans. De Putte, W. V.), 1961, *Complete Spiritual Doctrine of St Therese of Lisieux*, Alba House, New York.

Jung, C., 1951, *Fundamental questions of psychotherapy*, Princeton University Press, Princeton, NJ.

Kavanaugh, K. & Rodriguez, O., 1980, *The Collected Works of St Teresa of Avila*, vol. 2, ICS Publications, Washington.

Kearns, C. (Trans.), 1980, *The Life of Catherine of Siena by Raymond of Capua*, Dominican Publications, Dublin.

Kellerman, B., 2012, *The End of Leadership*, HarperBusiness, New York.

Komonchak, J.A., (ed), 2006, *History of Vatican II: The Council and the Transition; The Fourth Period and the End of the Council*, vol. V, Orbis, London – Peeters, Belgium.

Kouzes, J.M. & Posner, B.Z., 1987, *The Leadership Challenge*, Jossey-Bass, San Francisco.

Krasenbrink, J., 1996, *The Rupertsberg*. Retrieved 23 January 2014 from http://hildegard.org/wirk/erupert.html

Krznaric, R., 2012, "Six Habits of Highly Empathic People", *Greater Good*, 27 November. Retrieved 4 February 2015 from http://greatergood.berkeley.edu/article/item/six_habits_of_highly_empathic_people1

Lacoste, J.Y., (ed), 2005a, *Encyclopedia of Christian Theology*, vol. 1, Routledge, New York.

Lacoste, J.Y., (ed), 2005c, *Encyclopedia of Christian Theology*, vol. 3, Routledge, New York.

Lad, L.J. & Luechauer, D., 1998, "On the Path to Servant-Leadership", in *Insights on Leadership: Service, Stewardship, Spirit, and Servant-Leadership*, (ed), L. C. Spears, John Wiley & Sons, Inc., U.S.A., pp. 54-67.

Ladkin, D., 2010, *Rethinking leadership: A new look at old leadership questions*, Edward Elgar, Northampton, MA.

Lauter, W., 1996, *The Hildegardis Reliquary in the Eibingen Parish Church*. Retrieved 23 January 2014 from http://hildegard.org/wirk/eschrein.html

Lauter, W., 1996, *The Old Convent of Eibingen*. Retrieved 23 January 2014 from http://hildegard.org/wirk/eeibing.html

Lee, C., & Zemke, R., 1993, "The search for SPIRIT", *Workplace in Training*, June, 21-28.

Lewis, J. J., 2012, *Hildegard of Bingen Visionary, Composer, Writer* Retrieved 20 December 2012 from ://womenshistory.about.com/od/hildegard bingen/a/hildegard.htm

L'Osservatore Romano, 1970, *Doctor of the Church: A Reflection on Saint Teresa*, no. 40, (1 October) p. 1, p. 12.

L'Osservatore Romano, 2012, *What is Equivalent Canonization?* May 12.

L'Osservatore Romano, 2012, Weekly Edition in English, no.20 [2246], 16 May, p.11.

Marius, R. & Page, M.E., 2007, *A Short Guide to Writing About History*, Pearson Education, Inc., U.S.A.

McBrien, R., 1981, *Catholicism*, Study Edition, Winston Press, U.S.A.

McCuddy M.K. & Pirie, W.L., 2007, "Spirituality, stewardship, and financial decision-making Toward a theory of intertemporal stewardship", *Managerial Finance*, vol. 33, no. 12, pp. 957-969. Retrieved 16 September 2008 from Emerald database.

McGinn, B., 1999, *The Doctors of the Church: Thirty-Three Men and Women Who Shaped Christianity*, Crossword Publishing Company, New York.

Meagher, P.K. & O'Brien, T. C. & Aherne, C.M., (eds), 1979, "Encyclopedic Dictionary of Religion", *Corpus Publications*, Washington (vol. 1, vol. 2, vol. 3).

Medney, C., 2008, "Why empathy is as critical a skill as any other", *Advertising Age* (Midwest region edition), Chicago, Aug.11, vol.79, iss.31, p. 20. Retrieved 21 August 2008 from ProQuest database.

Middle Ages, 2015, *Anchoress*. Retrieved 29 March, 2015 from http://www.middle-ages.org.uk/anchoress.htm

Murphy, P.K. & Alexander, P.A., 2004, "Persuasion as a Dynamic, Multidimensional Process: An Investigation of Individual and Intraindividual Differences", *American Educational Research*, vol. 41, no. 2, summer, pp. 337-363. Retrieved 10 September, 2008 from JSTOR database.

Newman, B., 1990, "Introduction", in *Hildegard of Bingen: Scivias*, Hart, C. & Bishop, J. (Trans.) Paulist Press, U.S.A.

Newman, B., (ed), 1998, *Voice of the Living Light, Hildegard of Bingen and Her World*, University of California Press, California. U.S.A.

Noffke, S., 1980, *Catherine of Siena: The Dialogue*, Paulist Press, New Jersey. U.S.A.

Noffke, S., 2000, *The Letters of Catherine of Siena*, vol. 1, Center for Medieval and Renaissance Studies, Arizona, U.S.A.

Noffke, S., 2001, *The Letters of Catherine of Siena*, vol. 2, Center for Medieval and Renaissance Studies, Arizona, U.S.A.

Nouwen, H., 1979, *The Wounded Healer*, Image, Doubleday, New York.

O'Donnell, C., 1997, *Love in the Heart of the Church*, Veritas, Dublin.

O'Donnell, C., 2001, *Therese of Lisieux*, Veritas, Dublin.

O'Harae, I.S., 2007, "Beliefs shaping the practice of Christian school leadership: Implications for the principalship", *PhD Thesis*, CD-ROM, University of New England, Armidale.

O'Mahony, C., (ed & trans.), 1975, *St Therese of Lisieux by those who knew her: Testimonies from the process of beatification*, Veritas Publications, Dublin.

Palmer, P.J., 1998, "Leading from Within", in *Insights on Leadership: Service, Stewardship, Spirit, and Servant-Leadership*, (ed) L. C. Spears, John Wiley & Sons, Inc., U.S.A., pp. 197-208.

Palmer, R., 1969, *Hermeneutics*, North Western University Press, Evanston, IL.

Patenaude, W.L., 2014, The 'Green Pope' and a Human Ecology, *The Catholic Report*, April 22. Retrieved 15 May 2015 from: http://www.catholicworldreport.com/Item/3087/the_Green_Pope_and_a_Human_Ecology.

Patton, M.Q., 2002, *Qualitative Research and Evaluation Methods*, 3rd edn Sage Publications Inc, California.

Payne, S., 2002, *Saint Therese of Lisieux: Doctor of the Universal Church*, Alba House, Washington.

Peers, E.A. (ed & trans.), 1963a, *Saint Teresa of Jesus: The Complete Works*, vol. 1, the New Ark Library, Great Britain.

Peers, E.A. (ed & trans.), 1963b, *Saint Teresa of Jesus: The Complete Works*, vol. II, the New Ark Library, Great Britain.

Peers, E.A. (ed & trans), 1963c, *Saint Teresa of Jesus: The Complete Works*, vol. III, the New Ark Library, Great Britain.

Posa, C., 2012, "Hildegard: a woman for women and men of our times", *The Good Oil*, 20 November.

Rath, P., 1996, *Hildegard of Bingen Prophetess of her Time*. Retrieved on 23 January 2014 from http://hildegard.org/wirk/ehilde.html

Rath, P., 1996, *The New Abbey of St. Hildegard*. Retrieved 23 January 2014 from http://hildegard.org/wirk/eabtei.html

Rengers, C., 2000, *The 33 Doctors of the Church*, Tan Books and Publishers, inc. Illinois, U.S.A.

Rost, J.C., 1993, *Leadership for the Twenty-First Century*, Praeger Publishers, U.S.A.

Rough, D., 2011, *Leadership is Listening – Greenleaf Part 1*, January. Retrieved 5 February 2015 from: http://leadershipcache.blogspot.com.au/2011/01/leadership-is-listening-greenleaf-part.html

Rough, D., 2011, *Leadership is Persuasion – Greenleaf Part 5*, February. Retrieved 5 February 2015 from: http://leadershipcache.blogspot.com.au/2011/02/leadership-is-persuasion-greenleaf-pt-5.html

Rough, D., 2011, *Leadership is Commitment to the growth of people – Greenleaf Part 9*, May. Retrieved 5 February 2015 from: http://leadershipcache.blogspot.com.au/2011/05/commitment-to-growth-of-people.html

Russell, R.F., 2001, "The role of values in servant leadership," *Leadership and Organization Development*, vol. 22, no. 2, pp. 76-83. Retrieved 2008 from Emerald database.

Sadowski, D., 2015, "Preserving GOD'S CREATION", *Australian Catholic Weekly*, May 10, pp. 12-13.

Salem, R., 2003, "Empathic Listening", *Beyond Intractability*, July. Retrieved 12 February 2015 from: http://www.beyondintractability.org/essay/empathic-listening

Scaraffia, L., 2012, "The Equivalent Canonization of Hildegard of Bingen", *L'Osservatore Romano*, May 11.

Schein, E.H., 1999, "Empowerment, coersive persuasion and organizational learning: do they connect?", In *The Learning Organization*, vol. 6, no. 4, pp. 163-172. Retrieved 10 September 2008 from *Emerald* database.

Senge, M. P., "The Ecology of Leadership", *Leader to Leader*, no. 2, Fall. Retrieved on 19 February 2015 from: http://www.scribd.com/doc/95364454/Peter-Senge-Articles#scribd

Sequentia, 1994, "Canticles of Ecstasy: Hildegard of Bingen", *CD* BMG Music, New York, U.S.A.

Shula, D. & Blanchard, K., 1995, *Everyone's a Coach*, Harper Business & Zondervan Publishing House, New York & Grand Rapids, Mich.

Silvas, A., 1998, "Jutta and Hildegard: The Biographical Sources", *Medieval Women: Texts and Contexts*, University of Liverpool, Turnhout: Brepols, Belgium.

Silvas, A., 2012, "Saint Hildegard: Teutonic Prophetess, Sybil of the Rhine, Doctor of the Church", Talk given at the *Anima Conference*, November 3, 2012, Melbourne.

Sims, B.J., 1997, *Servanthood: Leadership for the Third Millennium*, Cowley Publications, U.S.A.

Spears, L.C., (ed), 1998, *Insights on Leadership: Service, Stewardship, Spirit, and Servant-Leadership*, John Wiley & Sons, Inc., U.S.A.

Spears, L.C., (ed), 1998, "Tracing the Growing Impact of Servant-Leadership", in *Insights on Leadership: Service, Stewardship, Spirit, and Servant-Leadership*, John Wiley & Sons, Inc., U.S.A.

Spears, L.C., 2010, "Character and Servant Leadership: Ten Characteristics of Effective, Caring Leaders", *The Journal of Virtues & Leadership*, vol.1, issue 1, pp. 25-30. Retrieved 5 February 2015 from: http://www.regent.edu/acad/global/publications/jvl/vol1_iss1/Spears_Final.pdf

Stogdill, R., 1974, *Handbook of Leadership: A survey of theory and research*, The Free Press, New York.

Stogdill, R., 1981, "Traits of leadership: A follow-up to 1970", in B. Bass (ed) *Stogdill's handbook of leadership*, pp. 73-97, Free Press, New York.

Stubbs, I. R., 1998, "A Leverage Force: Reflections on the Impact of Servant-Leadership", in *Insights on Leadership: Service, Stewardship, Spirit, and Servant-Leadership*, (ed) L. C. Spears, John Wiley & Sons, Inc., U.S.A., pp. 314-321.

Sturnick, J.A., 1998, "Healing leadership", in *Insights on Leadership: Service,*

Stewardship, Spirit, and Servant-Leadership, (ed) L.C. Spears, John Wiley & Sons, Inc., U.S.A., pp. 185-193.

Sutherland, E., 2010, "Hildegard of Bingen: Entry into Disibodenberg" [online]. *Parergon*, vol.27, no.1, 2010:53-66. Retrieved 28 March 2015 from: http://search.informit.com.au/documentSummary;dn=201007767;res=IELAPA ISSN: 0313-6221.

Taulbert, C.L., 2008, "Slow Down to Lead", *Leader to Leader*, vol. 2008, iss. 49, summer, pp. 36-40. Retrieved 19 September 2008 from ProQuest database.

Throop, P. (Trans.), 1998, *Hildegard von Bingen's PHYSICA The Complete English Translation of Her Classic work on Health and Healing*, Healing Arts Press, Rochester, Vermont.

Tromberend, T., 1996, *Bermersheim*. Retrieved 23 January 2014 from http://hildegard.org/wirk/ebermer.html

Trotta, Margarethe Von, 2010, *Vision – From the Life of Hildegard von Bingen*, DVD Zeitgeist video, Germany.

University of Maryland Medical System, 2013, *Thoughts and Reflections*, pp. 1-4. Retrieved 5 February 2015 from: http://umm.edu/patients/pastoral/thoughts-and-reflections

Vatican Radio, 2015, *Pope Francis approves the decrees for canonization of Louis and Zelie Martin*. 27 June. Retrieved from: http://www.news.va/en/news/pope-francis-approves-the-decrees-for-canonization

Volckmann, R., 2005, "An Interview with Joseph Rost", *Integral Leadership Review*, vol. 5, no. 3, July, 2005, pp. 1-15. Retrieved 3 Dec. 2007 from http://www.integralleadershipreview.com/archives/2005_07/2005_07_rost.html

Volckmann, R., 2012 (January/February 2015), "Integral Leadership and Diversity—Definitions, Distinctions and Implications", *Integral Leadership Review*. Retrieved from http://integralleadershipreview.com/7046-integral-leadership-and-diversity-definitions-distinctions-and-implications/

Weber, A., 1990, *Teresa of Avila and the Rhetoric of Femininity*, Princeton University Press, New Jersey, U.S.A.

Woodward, K.L., 1990, *Making Saints: How the Catholic Church Determines Who Becomes a Saint, Who Doesn't and Why*, Simon and Schuster, New York.

Yukl, G., 1989, *Leadership in Organizations*, Prentice-Hall, Englewood Cliffs, NJ.

Yukl, G., 2002, *Leadership in Organizations*, Prentice-Hall, Upper Saddle River.

www.ingramcontent.com/pod-product-compliance
Lightning Source LLC
Chambersburg PA
CBHW021855230426
43671CB00006B/402